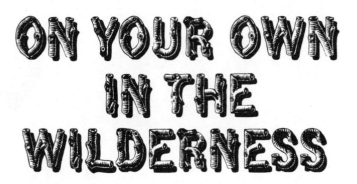

ON YOUR OWN IN THE WILDERNESS

BRADFORD ANGIER WITH COLONEL TOWNSEND WHELEN

Illustrated with photographs by the
authors and sketches by Vena Angier

HART PUBLISHING COMPANY, INC.
NEW YORK CITY

When Brad and I were writing this book, we were living 3,000 miles apart. He asked me to whom we should dedicate it.

I think it will be plain to every reader that there is one person to whom we owe much for her assistance, for helping to type and edit, for the contributions she has made, and by no means least for her inspiration.

So, entirely at my suggestion, this book is dedicated to

VENA ANGIER
a real wilderness wife.

Brad Angier

Contents

searching/evergreen bivouac/lean-to/
simplest form of campfire tent is a tarp

Colonel Townsend Whelen

1. The Return to the Land

This is October. Dark spruce greening the lower mountain-
sides are streaked with the gold of poplars. These stream
down the gullies to the parklike valley floor, where the little
willows the moose love so much have taken on their crimson
brightness. Among all this, shadows rise, extinguishing col-
or, as the sun is slowly sliced from sight by a saw-toothed
ridge. Its final rays momentarily ignite a snow peak to the
east with a startling ruby against the rich deep blue of the
Northern sky.

Our fire leaps at dry spruce logs, as the stars come out
one by one. The winds subside at this blending of the day
past with the night to come. All is hushed except for the
small noises of evening. Across a lake, ducks splash in the
reeds and quack softly. A great horned owl hoots—who-
who-who-ahew-hu-hu.

We eat our moose meat and bannock, sip our tea, and
gaze into the living warmth of the embers. Presently, like a
cool sough of air across a glacier, there breathes a sound:
softly, hesitantly, sadly at first, soaring and falling and lifting
again—a wolf singing of love, of the beauty of the silent
places, and of freedom. Over and over again *Mahheekun*

11

howls, so tenderly, sweetly, yearningly. Then we are alone
with the stillness.

This is our country. Does it call to you, too? Come with
us into it. Let us talk together about how to live in the wild.

Bradford Angier and I, Townsend Whelen, have had
much the same experiences, and this in a way is responsible
for our book . . .

Brad was a young Boston magazine editor and advertising executive with a background, starting even before his
teens, of year-around weekend camping throughout northern New England and summers of hiking, climbing, and
bivouacking in the North Woods. During these expeditions, he fell irretrievably under the spell of the quiet, the
beauty, and the peace of those almost unspoiled regions
where he built his lone campfires.

This deepening influence of the Farther Places later
impelled him to extend his regular holidays from advertising
and editorial duties with longer and still longer leaves of
absence. It was not long until a couple of months each year
he was hunting and fishing with his own little outfit on the
upper Southwest Miramichi River in New Brunswick, along
the Grand Cascapedia in the Gaspe's wild interior, and in
other wilderness expanses.

Finally, the love of nature at her best became an obses-
sion with him. Getting fed up with city-bound existence—
the artificiality, the crowds, the noise of Commonwealth
Avenue—he decided to make the break. He jumped off to
the wildest and one of the most beautiful spots in North
America—beyond the end of the last dirt wagon tracks,
where the wonderfully lonesome headwaters of the Peace
River plunge through the main chain of the Canadian Rockies. Arriving there in the middle of a sub-Arctic winter, he

settled down to a thoroughly happy log-cabin life on the sunny north bank of the otherwise vacant, never-navigated Rocky Mountain Canyon.

A century and a half before, Alexander Mackenzie had described that twenty-two-mile wilderness solitude as "one white sheet of foaming water." There, among hills lean with lodgepole pine and deep spruce-blued chasms, with a background of snow-coned peaks, Brad and his wife, Vena, continue to reside, living off the country and on the returns from their pens. Their occasional and only companions (and, it might be said, instructors) have been the frugal and competent hunters, trappers, prospectors, and men of Hudson's Bay Company, and their pioneer wives. From these sourdough individualists they have learned the art of living economically and comfortably in wild country, and of meeting every situation successfully with their brains and hands alone.

I, for my part, spent all of my boyhood summers in the Adirondack Mountains, hunting, fishing, and camping every clear day; and there I developed a love that passes all understanding for the uncut woods, the mountains, and the lakes. When I reached manhood, all my weekends and holidays found me in little pieces of God's country. Before very long, my readings about the Northwest and the illustrations I saw of its high, snow-capped peaks and its broad, deep valleys, together with the accounts of its game, so fired my imagination as to act like a lodestone.

So I, too, "jumped off" to the wildest and most glorious country I knew of—central British Columbia. That was in 1901, when I was twenty-three years of age. Departing from the end of the rails alone, with a saddle horse and two pack ponies loaded with grub and meager equipment, I started true north into an uninhabited country I knew nothing of—

not even how it looked on maps.

After a few days of wandering up valleys and over snow-covered passes, I came to the bivouac of an old hunter and prospector, one of the very last of the typical mountain men of the Old West, clad entirely in buckskin, long-haired, and looking as though he had stepped out of a painting by Remington. I camped that night with him. We took a liking to each other, and eventually we became partners to hunt, prospect, and trap in the wild regions to the north, where there was no civilization between us and the gold-stamped-ing horde which had recently rushed into the Yukon.

There we stuck together for nine glorious months, while that gigantic country cast on me the spell of the North that has remained ingrained in my soul ever since. At the start I was an "innocent pilgrim," but gradually Bones taught me the way of the mountains as only those of the Old West knew it: so very different, so much more efficient than the best methods of the Eastern guides—wilderness technique, we might say, which has all but disappeared.

Since those days, my forty years of service in our Army, including three wars, has afforded opportunity to learn the art of living in strange country and overcoming its obstacles. Leaves of absence and vacations invariably spent in the wilds have served to gratify and intensify my longings for the peace and freedom found only there.

Amateur exploration of these regions became my hobby. I usually went alone because finding my own way and overcoming all obstacles without assistance gave me an inexpressible thrill. Sometimes I had a congenial companion, or a canoeman, or a horse wrangler along. Only twice have I employed a guide, and then not to show me the way, but rather to permit more time for the intimate study of nature.

I have sometimes been called a "big-game hunter," but I dislike the term. I have been rather a wanderer in and worshiper of beautiful and unspoiled country, what some overcivilized and atrophied individuals call "the wastelands."

And so it was that Brad and I came to "savvy the bush."

Each of us, in the midst of our life in the open, became familiar with the classic writings on woodcraft of George W. Sears (Nessmuk) and Horace Kephart, and we also came under the spell of Thoreau's *Walden*. The works were inspirational and revealing, but unfortunately not even these writers knew real, wild, unspoiled country firsthand. Their personal experiences were confined to little stretches of wooded country almost within hearing of the steam whistle.

Wilderness expanse surrounding the Angiers' log cabin in British Columbia.

One of the rewards of a wilderness existence is the enjoyment of natural displays.

Most recent writers on life in the open have had rather limited experiences, and their works cover largely the ways of the modern sportsman tied to the apron strings of a guide, of boys' and girls' camp instruction, and of automobile and motorboat camping.

Gradually, it occurred to both of us that it was well worthwhile to put on record the old but time-tried ways of the wild before they were lost forever in a mass of modern technology. Our book would be based on experience we'd found to be the best ways of entering wild and unknown country, of finding one's own way through it, and of living there in comfort and safety, enjoying it to the utmost, and inviting one's soul.

When we started to live this life, there were no special manufactured conveniences such as exist today. There were not even fairly accurate maps of the wilder regions. Our first outfits were primitive—blankets, home kitchen utensils, ordinary grub, black-powder rifles, lumbermen's clothes, and little else.

Since then, the production of modern gadgets designed to help one take civilization into the wilderness has reached tremendous proportions. Much of this is just "junk with sales appeal," and in the words of the old-timers "not worth hellroom." However, certain pieces of modern equipment serve admirably to smooth the way, to make the outdoor life easier and more comfortable, to lighten the load, and to permit more time for the worship of nature. We have presented these items and explained their uses and advantages.

A lot of folks dream of escaping to some earthly paradise. Our hopes are that what we have written here may help some of them make that dream come true. Try it first for a holiday. Possibly afterwards you may jump off for good. What Thoreau proved more than a century ago about returning to nature will still work today.

2. Outdoor Outfits and Outfitters

At the turn of the century, there was no such thing as a sportsman's outfitter. There were not even very many big-game hunters in the strictest sense of the term, although not a few adventurers stampeded throughout the Yukon, British Columbia, and Alaska as much in hope of bagging moose and grizzly as of finding gold.

Many rangers, lumbermen, farmers, and others close to the outdoors hunted in the localities near to them. But most of our city men who could afford long wilderness trips were too busy making money. Comparatively few sportsmen hunted far afield, although this has become commonplace today. It was not until about 1900, as a matter of fact, that the Alaska brown bear and the Rocky Mountain goat became generally known among our North American big-game animals.

In the East about that time were a number of young college graduates, usually sons of rich fathers, who had spent their boyhood summers at camps in and around Maine and the Adirondacks. Here they had learned to love the woods. These young men, more or less under the influence of Theodore Roosevelt and his writings, began to turn their eyes farther afield to wilder country, to the West and to the Canadian wilds. They formed the vanguard of our present-day phalanx of trophy hunters.

In those days, when adventurous young men wanted to hunt or fish in far regions not known to them, they customarily hired a guide. This guide was perhaps a trapper, a logger, a miner, or a cattleman who knew his own particular wilderness. He furnished the sportsman with his personal things, his blankets, and his ax. In the West, he often supplied packhorses and rigging as well. In river and lake country, he many times provided canoe, paddles, poles, and the like.

The sportsman saw to nearly everything else—tents, bedding, cooking and eating utensils, and the food. In fact, he usually brought most of this outfit with him from the city.

From about 1898, sporting-goods stores in the great cities such as Boston, New York, Chicago, and San Francisco began to furnish outfits to the growing number of outdoorsmen. There were tents of various kinds, duffel bags of one sort and another, grub sacks, a variety of blankets, and shortly thereafter the newly contrived sleeping bags, which immediately provoked a stampede of adverse comment and sour looks, especially among old-timers. A lot of this particular disfavor stemmed legitimately from the earlier sleeping contraptions themselves, particularly those with waterproof covers which soon rendered all contents, including the occupant, clammy with retained moisture.

The Standard Cooking and Eating Utensil Kit

These stores also rigged up a set of aluminum cooking and eating utensils that was so good that it has persisted as a sort of standard up to the present day. A kit consisted generally of some three nested aluminum kettles with bails. Inside the smallest kettle went three or so aluminum soup bowls, as well as an equal number of enamel cups; these had handles that were open at the bottom so that they also would stack one inside the other. Room remained for table knives, forks, spoons, a short butcher knife, a spatula, a dish mop, salt and pepper shakers, and so on, not forgetting the can opener, inevitable even then. Nine-inch and twelve-inch frypans with detachable handles fitted on the bottom of the nested kettles, along with aluminum plates. The entire outfit packed into a canvas bag twelve inches high and wide. There were also such auxiliary items which could be purchased separately, such as folding aluminum reflector bakers and mixing pans.

You can still secure all these articles either in sets or individually, substituting if you want stainless steel cups for the still popular enamel. In any event, it is wise to avoid aluminum cups, which are as hot to drink from as a tomato can. In general, no better outfit has ever been devised for the outdoor purpose for which it was designed. This is not true of considerable other outdoor equipment.

I bought a full outfit of this kind when I first started west in 1901. Arriving at my jumping-off spot, which happened to be Ashcroft, British Columbia, I purchased a riding-horse, two packhorses, and saddles. I packed my belongings and grub on the animals and started north alone; in the interest of self-preservation, I grew quite familiar with such a rig.

The cooking kit, it so happens, lasted me intact until 1916. Then a *cayuca*, a dugout canoe, in which I was cruising along the Caribbean coast, got swamped. Everything that I owned went to the bottom except my rifle. But that is another story.

Soon afterward I duplicated the cooking outfit, and it

has lasted me ever since. It's still serviceable, and has gone with me on every trip where transportation was adequate. Brad, too, has had one he has happily used for the past 40 years.

Outdoor Trips in the Old Days

A fishing or hunting foray into the wilds during those early years was relaxingly primitive. In the West, your guide often took along a helper who combined the jobs of cook and wrangler. The guide charged about five dollars a day for himself and maybe three dollars for his hired help. He collected another dollar apiece daily for saddle horses and half that amount for pack cayuses.

You furnished the grub and most of the outfit. You did as much work as anyone else and maybe a little more. The guide showed the way into game country, and you hunted alone. On moving days, all hands packed and rustled the animals.

Cooking was done over an open fire except when you ran into a top hand with a Dutch oven. In this case, the only difference was that he sometimes buried the heavy utensil underground in a safe place where fire would not spread, with plenty of glowing embers above and below. On other occasions, he just set the Dutch oven among hot wood coals, some of which he raked over the top. These cooking fires were usually built in front of a large tarpaulin that was pitched as a lean-to.

Your guide in the Northeast charged about the same, but usually threw in his canoe without extra cost. When there was a party, each sportsman customarily had a guide or the cook in his canoe. You had to be more or less able to handle this type of watercraft—although, as is the case today, you could serve an apprenticeship at the bow paddle.

You helped over the portages. You pitched in with the various camp chores. You earned your sport, and took a just pride in the ability you acquired to care for yourself afield under any and all conditions.

Colonel Whelen bagging a moose in New Brunswick.

Modern Outfitters

Times have changed since then. Today's big-game hunter usually hasn't been schooled in the camps of northern New England, the Adirondacks, and the Sierra. In the main, the hunters and fishermen who can afford to travel to the increasingly distant forests and streams of our shrinking frontiers are successful professional and businessmen; on their first trips, they generally know little or nothing about either wilderness life or outdoor living. Most are in a hurry.

Many of them, for one reason or another, expect to be cared for in every way imaginable. Not a few consider as their rights certain luxuries that the old-timers not only never dreamed of but would scoff at.

And so the sportsman's outfitter has been born. He has crews of guides, cooks, bull cooks, wranglers, and packers, and complete outfits of horses, saddles, panniers, and so on; or canoes with outboard motors and boats with inboard motors; or trucks, jeeps, station wagons, trail bikes, snowmobiles, and various types of aircraft. You need only provide your personal belongings, your time, and usually your firearms and rods (though the latter can be rented instead). You have to give little thought to anything beyond arriving at a specified place at an agreed upon time.

Depending on where you go and how you travel, you will be provided with a cabin, or possibly a bedroom, or maybe a personal tent. In cold weather, steps will be taken to warm your quarters before you turn out in the morning.

On pack-train trips, for example, there will be a dining tent and often a separate cook tent with its own stove. Meals will include fresh bread and pie and cake baked in a real oven, heavy canned goods, and numerous delicacies—even to caviar and pate de foie gras. All this will have been previously okayed by the client from lengthy grub lists customarily mailed to him well in advance.

Gone are the old Three-B days of beans, bacon, and bannock. Gone, more regrettably, is the wilderness life. Civilization has taken to the woods.

For all this organized service, the outfitter will probably charge you about $100 a day for extended trips with a pack train. In the extreme Northwest and Alaska, expenses and therefore rates run higher. Trophy hunting in the remoter regions of this continent is now pretty much a rich man's game.

This, in general, is the system today, and at first glance it looks mighty rough for the individual of modest means who longs for the freedom and the scope of the primitive wilds. The more helpers, animals, stoves, tents, and other equipment the outfitter supplies, the more he must charge. If you don't want all this assistance, there are plenty of others who do and will pay for it. By May, nearly every good outfitter has all his dates secured by deposits for the entire forthcoming season. Furthermore, in many of the more desirable hunting localities, local laws require that a nonresident be accompanied by a registered guide.

As far as the outfitter is concerned, this in all fairness should be added: throughout the continent, we happen to know a large number of outfitters personally, not one of whom is putting much money away. Most of them have to maintain very costly and quickly depreciating outfits, replacements for which come increasingly high. The income-producing seasons are comparatively brief.

It seems to us old-timers that on fully outfitted trips you don't see or learn much about the genuine lure of the outdoors. You don't get to taste the peace, the contentment, the warm realization of adequacy, and the deep-seated sportsmanship that are revealed only to those who personally come to grips with the farther places. To us old fellows, all these things fall within the list of the passions that cannot be translated into words.

The Advantages of Self-Reliance

Despite all the encroachments of civilization, the wilderness is still a great educator and leavener. The Western dude or the Eastern sport who starts under these present comparatively luxurious conditions does not long remain a tenderfoot. Either he quits the game when he has a few heads to hang on his wall, or he becomes a real hunter, fisherman, and woodsman in his own right.

If you have red blood in your veins, a love for the beautiful, and a deep-down yearning for freedom and peace, you soon learn to do things for yourself. You take a more and more justifiable pride in your increasing competence. Perhaps you start out hardly able to step over a picket rope and end by hurdling the mountain.

As for the "good old days" that a lot of folks talk about, there are still thousands of square miles in North America alone that have never even been walked on.

At Home in the Woods

There is another way to answer the lure of the wilderness. It is the way my writing partner took.

British Columbia challenged Brad, as it had challenged

me years before. He was not able to afford an outfitter, guide, and pack train. What he did was pack his outfit in duffel bags and head for a nearly vacant place on the map. For most of the last forty years he has hunted, fished, camped, prospected, ridden his own horses, and lived in a log cabin on the Peace River where this wilderness stream bursts through the Rocky Mountains on its journey to the Arctic Ocean.

Why, ask readers of *Living off the Country, How to Build Your Home in the Woods, Field Guide to Edible Wild Plants,* and his over two dozen other books, did he so abruptly quit his media career to go to the woods? As a matter of fact, the transition wasn't so abrupt. Like a lot of others, he had been putting off going for a long time. What finally decided him was a remark Henry Thoreau made over a century earlier after living two years in the woods: "If you have built castles in the air, your work need not be lost. That is where they should be. Now put the foundations under them."

Nowhere but there at Hudson Hope, he and his wife have long since decided, can ever be their real home— where they can live deep and suck out all the marrow of life. A gasoline lantern is their lighting works, a pair of pails their water system. There are other inconveniences, too. Well, maybe some folks would call them that; the Angiers did, too, before they realized these are also freedoms. If one doesn't have running water, there's no worry about meters and bursting pipes. If stoves crackle with your own wood, high fuel costs and labor-management difficulties are something to plague the other fellow.

They learned this by their experiment: if you advance confidently in the direction of your dreams and endeavor to lead the life which you have imagined, you will meet with a success unexpected in common hours.

People have more leisure than ever before. Not many years ago numerous men accepted as incontrovertible fact the pattern of working hard all their lives in order to be able to retire some day to the uncrowded places. The months of countless others were measured by the few days they could snatch from each harried year for the brief ecstasy of camping, fishing, hunting, or just plain rusticating.

Now the five-day, thirty-five or forty-hour week is commonplace. So are longer and longer weekends and annual vacations. Combined with all these are increasingly swifter and cheaper forms of transportation to whisk you where you will.

The Rocky Mountain Canyon in which the Angiers' home in the woods is located.

The Fun of Assembling Your Own Outfit

What you will need if you are going to take fullest possible advantage of the woods, hills, and streams is, obviously, an outfit of your own. Not only is assembling such a rig one of the most enduring joys of the outdoorsman's life, but only when you are equipped to camp by yourself will you be in line to lead the simple life to the fullest.

The secret of being miserable is to have the leisure to bother about whether you are happy or not. This is one reason why for many individuals the most pleasurable hours of the weeks and months when they're barred from the forests and lakes are those during which they go over their outfits.

There are always a few items which, because they were not used during the last trip or even on the one before, you—being a reasonable man—regretfully relegate to the closet. Perhaps, it must be admitted, most of them are returned to the active pile during those moments of weakness, or lucidity, that are almost sure to intervene before the next excursion.

Then there are always those essentials without which you can do no longer, no matter what their purchase does to the budget. After you have gone through the process of adding, discarding, and reconsiderng for years, you will have to admit even to yourself that there is no such thing as a perfect outfit. However, trying to achieve the near ideal is all the more challenging for that.

One advantage of the primitive life is that it teaches one what are the necessaries. Most of the luxuries and many of the so-called comforts are not only dispensable, but positive hindrances. Our life is frittered away with detail. To maintain one's self on this earth is not a hardship but a pastime, if we will live simply and wisely. As Thoreau said, "a man is rich in proportion to what he can do without."

Evaluating New Methods with an Open Mind

A lot has happened since I first hit the trail. Scurvy, which was still taking a lot of outdoorsmen in those early days, we now know can be simply conquered without the cost of a single penny. Insect repellents that really work are available; these have it all over the old tarry, smelly, and ineffective dopes. All the shelter necessary for many an outdoor trip can now be carried in a shirt pocket.

On the other hand, good wool socks have not only never been surpassed, but they are still the only ones satisfactory for hiking. There are still a few very good boots, and a lot of downright harmful ones. Much of the outdoor clothing made from synthetic fabrics is uncomfortable and even dangerous to wear. Some of the nylon tents can freeze you to death. Plastic dishes are no equal for the familiar old nested aluminum and steel favorites.

Techniques have been improved. However, that most conservative of all classes—we outdoorsmen—do not always learn of these changes. For example, in an article for one of the big outdoor magazines, I had this to say about the proper positioning of the backpack: "The pack sags down into the hollow of your back and over half its weight rests on your hips. The notion that the pack weight should be carried high up on your shoulders is all wet." This observation drew the following intelligent, courteous and, incidentally, characteristic letter. After quoting the above passage from my article, the reader wrote: "We now turn to what is practically

The Colonel's grandson, Townsend Whelen Bowling, demonstrates the proper positioning of an Alpine frame rucksack: the pack sags down into the hollow of the back, with over half its weight resting on the hips.

Holy Writ for the outdoorsman. Kephart states, 'Worse still, the pack rides so low that it presses hard against the small of the back, which is the worst of all places to put a strain on.' And speaking of the *Nessmuk* packsack, 'This packsack carries higher, and hence more comfortably, than a rucksack.' It would be blatant impudence on my part ot criticize any of these [Kephart's, Nessmuk's, and Whelen's] statements. But I would be less confused if someone would equate all the above excerpts!"

My answer was: "I fear the authorities you quote on

backpacking are rather out of date. Nessmuk's *Woodcraft* dates back about 65 years, and Kephart's *Camping and Woodcraft* about forty years. Lots of water has gone over the dam since then. . . .

"Backpacking is still being done over the whole world wherever there is country without road and river communications. In each locality the method is different, or at least slightly so. . . . But there is no locality where so much attention has been given to backpacking by fairly educated men of ingenuity and resourcefulness as that country in our western mountains from northern California clear to the Arctic Ocean, and also among Alpinists the world over who climb high peaks for sport.

"Here these men of long experience—hunters, trappers, prospectors, and sportsmen—have, in recent years, come in almost all cases to prefer either the Alaska packboard or the Bergans type of Alpine frame rucksack, and they invariably let the shoulder straps out so these packs sag down slightly. I have done most of my packing in this country (and in the wilder portions of Panama). I have been more or less associated with these men, and I have adopted their method because it has proved best.

"If you tighten the shoulder straps on a pack so it rides high on the shoulders, the weight is both on top and on the front of your shoulders. The weight and pressure of the shoulder straps on the front of your shoulders tend to pull you backward. So you lean forward, and tighten up your stomach muscles, and this to some extent interferes with your breathing. The shoulder straps are so tight they cut into your shoulders. The weight, being carried high, tends to make you top-heavy, and you are not as surefooted. You have more or less trouble getting your arms through the straps and the pack up on your shoulders where it must be.

"If you let the shoulder straps out slightly so the pack sags down a little toward and almost on the hips, then the weight comes almost on the front of the shoulders, and the pack does not pull you backward. The pack being lower, your center of gravity is lower. You are in better balance, and you are more sure-footed. It is far easier to put the pack on your shoulders and your arms through the straps. It's just like putting on and taking off a pair of suspenders."

As each of us observes the world from a different trail, it is only natural that points of view will vary, as mine did from those of Kephart and Nessmuk. Take for example three sportsmen approaching a water hole. One will see only the disappearing cubs. Another will see only the large bear hurrying nearer. The third will see both cubs and mother. All three will have seen what they were looking at, and all three will have been right.

Brad and I do not, for a moment, suppose that our ways are the only ways, but we trust that our observations will be helpful.

3. A Great Camping Area

Do you want a great new experience in camping? Throughout all tropical America, from central Mexico to southern Brazil, you will find vast stretches of unspoiled and practically uninhabited wilderness. Part of this is in grass and plains. Other portions are dense with thickets of so-called second growth. The biggest segment, however, is the primeval rain forest thought of by most northerners as jungle.

The Tropical Rain Forest

Actually, this is a true forest not much denser than many in the eastern United States, but with exotic growth and with many trees of remarkable size that stretch up and up before spreading their tops and hiding the sky. Beneath this canopy, it is shady and cool. There is little underbrush, only some small palms and plants.

This is a entirely different world from what most northern sportsmen are used to. It shelters a multitude of animals, birds, and freshwater fish that are more or less strange to the majority of us. All, incidentally, are good to eat.

The deer of the tropics are small.

This rain forest may not be particularly attractive to a hunter interested only in big game. The only fairly large animals are small deer, peccary, tapir, puma, and jaguar. These are all somewhat difficult to find, see, or hunt in the prevalent cover. But here you will find many species of small mammals, more birds than anywhere else in the world, and an exciting abundance of fish in the streams.

Nor is this a region for sportsmen who expect to have their work done for them. There are few outfitters, guides, or even camp helpers. But if you are a lover of nature and if you like to wander on your own through wild and unspoiled country, the ancient wilderness of tropical America has a particular fascination.

Moreover, the rain forest is the easiest type of country that I know for camping and roaming. You can siwash there almost indefinitely, living off the land at scarcely any expense. The most valuable element, as a matter of fact, will be your time. You'll find yourself becoming stingy with every hour.

It is always summer here in the tropics. The climate within the prehistoric rain forest, however, is not nearly so hot and humid as that of many of our own southern states. And contrary to usually accepted notions, the forest is as health-sustaining as any place in the world.

It is entirely practical to enter this pristine wonderland with no more than you can easily pack on your back, to hunt and fish and photograph and live with nature for almost as long as you will, and all in all to have a glorious and totally different adventure that you'll never forget.

I know, for I have spent two years in doing just that.

The dry season and the wet season are the only seasons hereabouts. The arrival and the duration of these differ in various localities. You will naturally take them into account when making your plans. The vacationist will ordinarily prefer the dry months, of course, when it hardly ever rains. But, actually, the only difficulty that rainy weather presents is that of finding dry firewood.

For either season, only a very few precautions need to be taken, even less now than when I was there because of the tremendous advances in medicine during the past few years. Some of these simple safeguards are discussed in Brad's and Dr. Russ Kodet's *Being Your Own Wilderness Doctor*. Your physician can advise you of others. At night, you should camp at least a mile from any native habitation so as to avoid mosquitoes that may be infected with malaria. You should always have a mosquito bar for the night; malaria carriers do not attack until sunset. Any skin abrasion or cut should get prompt attention.

As this country is largely uninhabited, the water is likely to be pure. However, it is always well, any place in the world, to take the usual brief precautions with drinking water that are considered in detail in the last chapter. Rivers and small streams are found almost everywhere. A bath every evening followed by a change of underwear is, therefore, less a chore than a pleasantly awaited refreshment—and highly desirable.

Climate and terrain make it an easy matter to camp, travel, and live in comfort with a surprising minimum of effort. Not even bedding, which in the north comprises the heaviest and bulkiest essential camp gear, is needed here. Only the lightest shelter is required. There is even usable firewood everywhere that does not have to be cut.

Packing

You have your choice of two ways of traveling and living in this country. The first is to go afoot and pack everything on your back. This procedure sounds like a lot of work. Really, there is no way easier. Then you are absolutely footloose and free to roam wherever you like. Foot travel with a thirty-five-pound backpack is just as uncomplicated and practical here as in our own Appalachian and Pacific Coast regions, where thousands of more or less inexperienced campers and hikers do it every year.

Since you largely eliminate bedding and shelter in the ordinary sense, your basic outfit is amazingly light and compact. This permits you to carry some twenty to twenty-five pounds of store grub. Hunting and fishing along the way, you can make journeys or sojourns of up to a month and more, independent of all commercial sources of supply.

Excellent packs are the frame rucksacks of the Alpine

type and the packboard. These don't heat up your back. They are so adaptable that with them you can carry almost any weight or type of outfit.

For combined bedding and shelter, you have a mosquito bar about seven by three by three feet. To the bottom of this is sewed a light waterproof ground cloth. This is left loose on one side so that you can crawl under the netting, then tuck it beneath the floor cloth to make a mosquitoproof and antproof shelter. Over all this is stretched the lightest fly you can get, possibly a section of plastic sheeting weighing three or four ounces.

To pitch camp, merely clear off a piece of flat ground, cut a dozen of the large palm fronds which are everywhere, haul them to the cleared place, and then with your machete lop off leaflets until they pile a foot deep. Stake down the ground cloth over this heap, and the green stuff mats down to a springy mattress six inches hick.

Support the corners of your mosquito bar with sticks, stretch the fly over all, and your camp is up. At night you crawl inside, strip off your clothing, and go to sleep on the floor cloth. I invariably slept raw, but one or two of my men preferred an ordinary sheet for cover.

A minimum of cooking and eating utensils will suffice, such as two small nesting pots, a frypan with folding handle, an enamel or stainless steel cup, and a few implements. You'll need a tiny first-aid outfit and a small toilet kit, as well as a few personal items. Pack a machete instead of an ax, the latter being entirely unnecessary here. With the bedding, this is all the basic outfit you will need or can reasonably use. It shouldn't weigh more than ten pounds including the pack, and you'll still have plenty of room to stick in this book if you want.

For food, take mostly items such as flour, cereals, edible

In the tropics, a light pack will suffice, since less provisions for shelter and bedding are necessary.

fats not requiring refrigeraton, salt, sugar, baking powder, powdered milk and eggs, instant tea or coffee, dried fruit, and so on—in other words, grub that goes well with fish and game. As an emergency ration, you may care to include two pounds of rice. With all that, matches, compass, fishing and hunting equipment, and a good light knife, you can live in the rain forest for a long time.

For your sporting outfit, I would suggest a rifle for a load like the .22 Hornet, with a supply of full-charge cartridges for the larger game and, for smaller prey, reduced loads having ballistics similar to those of the .22 Long Rifle cartridge. You'll also want fishline, snell hooks, and sinkers. A good 35-mm. camera, film in sealed waterproof cans, a small exposure meter, a tiny clamp holding device, red and yellow and polarizing filters, and a self-timer will also be very desirable.

All you need in the way of clothing are khaki trousers and shirt, summer underwear, a broad-brimmed hat, and sneakers with six-inch canvas tops. The sneakers will last from two weeks to a month depending on how much you wade in streams. Take a change of underwear and several pairs of light woolen socks, and each evening wash the ones you have worn during the day.

By Dugout Canoe

If backpacking doesn't appeal to you, the other way to enter such country is by dugout canoe. You can paddle, pole, wade, and occasionally line your cayuca up one of the smaller rivers that uncoil like lustrous threads from the uninhabited country.

On such a trip you can take more equipment and grub. You can also substitute a jungle hammock for the previously described shelter. The hammock, though, is too heavy and bulky for backpacking. Furthermore, it is no more comfortable than a mosquito bar, nor is it easier to erect. Its bottom is a canvas sheet. Above this, rope supports a waterproof fly with net sides which overlap each other on the hammock to provide a mosquitoproof enclosure.

Don't get the idea, however, that mosquitoes infest this area in great numbers. They all fly by night only, and you'll rarely run into more mosquitoes than might make for potentially annoying sleep. As for snakes and venomous reptiles, they are no more plentiful than in our own South.

Don't forget a compass. Often you won't be able to see the sun for hours because of the leafy ceiling overhead. Your compass is very necessary, too, for keeping oriented in cloudy weather. In a level area you might walk in circles and easily get lost. Often in such terrain I have found it necessary to keep a scratch map of my route, orienting and drawing in the trail in back of me every mile or fifteen minutes, so I would know exactly where I had been and would be able to follow my route back.

If you keep your outfit with you always, you may *elect* to get lost—keeping track of your whereabouts only to such a measure as would enable you to steer your way back to civilization within some four or five days, or when your trip nears its end.

When you come out, what a tale you will have to tell about this entirely different world you have been in. Anyone who has sat by a campfire at night in the jungle wilderness wants to go back. I hope that someday I can.

Such a trip naturally takes careful planning. You can handle the details yourself, or get help from a travel agency. If you're doing the job on your own, a good way to start is either by writing directly to the country you're interested in, or by visiting or otherwise getting in touch with one of its local consulates. If none is in your area, write the consulate in Washington or in New York City. You will probably wish to ask for information on any regulations covering hunting, the bringing in of firearms, fishing, camping, and traveling in general. You may want to know if native helpers are available.

And when your planning is done and you are ready to head into the tropical mountains and valleys, you will be in for adventure and sport that's different from anything you've ever known.

4. Backpacking Vacations

Backpacking is one of the pleasantest ways of spending a vacation in the open. It has two advantages over all other ways of vacationing afield. *First:* since you carry all necessary equipment on your back, you are absolutely footloose, free, and independent to roam and pitch your shelter where you will. You need to rely on no one, and you have none of the bother and expense of automobiles, boats, and pack animals. *Second:* it is the cheapest of all ways of vacationing. Once you have assembled your small and inexpensive outfit and have arrived at your jumping-off place, you can hunt, fish, and prospect at no expense other than for food—for less than it costs to live at home, especially if you take along such a book as Brad's *Feasting Free on Wild Edibles* or *Field Guide to Edible Wild Plants.*

There is nothing particularly new about backpacking. Our early frontiersmen traveled that way whenever they entered the wilderness. Daniel Boone spent two whole years more or less alone in the virgin wilderness of Kentucky, living off the country, with no outfit except that which he had been carrying when he left.

Modern equipment and improved methods have been developed that rid the pastime of its drudgery and hard physical work. It will pay us to look carefully at these methods and equipment, for they are based on experience. Those who have never done any backpacking in the right manner with a good outfit have the idea that it is the toughest kind of toil. We often hear the expression, "I don't propose to make a packhorse of myself!" It is a lamentable fact that about half of those who attempt such a vacation never repeat it because they have found it too much like hard work—and all because of improper equipment and mistaken technique.

Done right, there is nothing hard about backpacking. Two things only are essential: fresh water, which you can purify if you must, and country where you can pitch camp without trespassing. Carrying your all on your back, you can journey into any sparsely settled and well-watered country. Such land is not hard to find in any region of the U. S., even in range of the big cities. Three hours drive or less will transport you away from the noise and the crowds of, say, New York or Washington to the natural delights of the Catskill Mountains or the Shenandoah Valley.

Maximum Loads

A basic consideration is how much weight we can carry, all day long if necessary, over the fairly rough and perhaps steep trails we may strike in wilder terrain. Typical country of this sort is encountered on the Appalachian and the Pacific Crest trails.

It is on these proving grounds that experienced and

enthusiastic outdoorsmen have developed a modern technique vastly superior to older haphazard methods. These procedures are thoroughly in accord with the modern practices of scalers of the world's loftiest mountains. They coincide, too, with the down-to-earth practices of the hardy trappers, prospectors, and hunters of the really wild and remote regions of Alaska, British Columbia, the Yukon and Northwest Territories, and the jungle country of Central and South America.

All this experience has clearly indicated that a young, vigorous, and athletic man should not attempt a backload of over thirty-five pounds for his first year or two of packing over fairly rough country. This is for hikes of two or more days, averaging from five to fifteen miles a day in fairly good weather. After the first year or two, his own experience will be his guide as to how much he can pack without undue fatigue. The limit for the similarly vigorous and athletic young woman is about twenty-five pounds.

These weights must be graded for others, as youth, age, and physical condition impose limitations. These considerations are for all-day hiking; they have no reference to what may be possible for one to pack a few miles to a more or less permanent camp, or the loads that can be wrestled a mile or so across a canoe portage.

In the past, almost every hiker has overloaded himself, at least at first, under the impression that he needed a lot of stuff if he were to avoid hardships. But if you take the right articles and use them in the right way, there are no hardships. The two slogans every backpacker should adopt are: (1) "Go light but right," and (2) "When in doubt, leave it out." As to the proper positioning of the backpack, see pages 29-32 for my response to a perplexed outdoorsman.

The experienced backpacker knows the maximum weight he can carry without fatigue; the novice, provided he is young and healthy, should keep his backload under thirty-five pounds.

Mileage

Mileage depends on such factors as the roughness and steepness of the trail, the climate, and particularly the temperature. Experienced hikers of average physique, carrying a pack of a weight commensurate with their capabilities, should average from two to fifteen miles a day in dry, reasonably cool weather. This they should do without becoming exhausted to a point where hiking is no longer a recreation. At the end of the hike, they should arrive in condition to make an agreeable camp and to enjoy their supper and a wholesome night's rest.

Never press if you can avoid it. Some days you may be up against an exceedingly steep and hard climb up a mountain the first thing in the morning. The two-mile struggle to the top may leave you dripping with sweat and feeling quite exhausted. If you are in good physical condition, a short rest will be all it will take to make you feel tops again. But after such an exertion it will usually be unwise to attempt more that day, and you had better stop and camp at the first half-decent spot. On the other hand, on a fine brisk day over a good trail, fifteen miles may be just a delightful jaunt, particularly if the scenery is stimulating.

The Basic Pack

In dry temperate weather, a hiker on lonely trails can get along all right for a night or so lying by a fire without bedding or shelter and eating food either uncooked or roasted on a forked stick. But on an extended trip he must carry an outfit which will insure adequate protection from rain and wind, undisturbed sleep, and good nourishing meals. Anything less than this spells discomfort, needlessly wasted energy, possible injury to health and, decidedly, no fun.

The experience of those who have long specialized in backpacking indicates that for summer and early fall the lightest practical camp and trail outfit, not including food, will weigh about fifteen pounds. For colder weather, where night temperatures approach zero, the basic weight should be increased by an additional two pounds of goosedown insulation in the sleeping bag.

Your basic pack should contain all the necessary provisions for shelter, warmth, dryness, comfort, and for the preparation and eating of meals. If the total load is going to be limited to thirty pounds, for example, this will then permit the carrying of fifteen pounds of food.

To maintain energy, a stalwart individual, doing hard outdoor work such as hiking and backpacking, needs just about two and a quarter pounds of well-selected and reasonably water-free grub per day. If the hiking country through which one journeys does not permit replenishment of food, fifteen pounds of provisions will suffice for seven days, not including breakfast at the start of the first day. In other words, with a total load of thirty pounds, the amount of food that can be included limits the duration of one's trip to about one week.

This week can be extended almost without limit if there are stores, towns, or farms along the trail where victuals can be restocked from time to time as needed. Such supply points exist every ten to thirty miles along many of our more popular hiking ways, either alongside the particular route or a mile or so off it.

The backpacker can also take advantage of the fact that in a wilderness, laws permitting, he can replenish his food not only with wild fruits and vegetables as he goes along, but also with fish and game. If a man is a competent woodsman, hunter, and fisherman, he can thrive indefinitely in a good game country on fat rare meat alone, and yet maintain perfect health and vigor.

The basic outfit should then include the firearm most suitable to the region, sufficient ammunition, fishhooks or a fish net, snare wire, and an adequate supply of matches. Clothing, as it is worn out, can be replaced from the skins of the animals secured. Not even salt is essential. After you've gone without salt for a few weeks, you'll very possibly lose your appetite for it, even after you've tried it again.

Essential Shelter

Some kind of shelter is usually essential for overnight camps as protection from rain, wind, and possibly even snow or mosquitoes. As a matter of fact, you sometimes get the last two together. A tent is the usual form of shelter from the elements. One outfitter furnishes a waterproof and bugproof tent, intended for Alpinists and backpackers, that weighs three pounds, tapers from forty-five to thirty-six inches in height, is just seven feet long, and is quite reasonable. In some country, and during some seasons, such a piece of equipment is a fine thing to have along.

However, the expense and weight of a tent can be dispensed with in almost all temperate North America from the middle of June through the first half of September. One's bed can be sheltered instead with a simple tarpaulin, about five feet by seven feet, stretched as a lean-to with its back toward the direction from which storms are likely to come. For cheerful warmth, a fire built five feet or so in front of such a lean-to will reflect light and heat into it.

Such a tarp, made of nylon or very light plastic sheeting, need weigh only a few ounces. The commercial plastic poncho, obtainable from most dealers in camp supplies, measuring sixty-six inches by ninety inches and weighing fifteen ounces, is excellent for this purpose. It will also serve as a raincoat, covering both person and pack. It can be used, too, below the bedding to keep out dampness from the ground. In the unlikely event of a wind that blows the rain into the lean-to, the bed can be protected by a roof of spruce boughs thrown up in front of the shelter which will cause the drops to fall straight down instead of driving in on the bed.

Such an arrangement makes a very practical and comfortable bivouac at savings of about thirty dollars and two and one-half pounds, as compared to the previously mentioned tent.

BEDDING

Your bed will be the bulkiest and heaviest article in your pack. In summer weather, when night temperatures do not ordinarily go below 45° Fahrenheit, a mummy bag weighing about two pounds will suffice for more sturdy outdoor individuals.

There are two secrets for keeping warm on cool nights with light bedding. One is to turn in dry and fully clothed, except for shoes. Garments and bedding can, of course, be dried before the campfire if necessary. The other prerequisite is to have a soft mattress so that one's weight will press only a minimum of the insulating dead air out of the coverings. This mattress can be made of spruce or other evergreen boughs, shingled on the bed space as described in chapter 11. Pine needles, leaves, or grass gathered close by can also be used. Then, too, a plastic air mattress is available in sections each two feet square and each weighing fourteen ounces. Two sections snapped together make a mattress twenty-four by forty-eight inches, which is ample. While this means additional weight of nearly two pounds, plus some bulk, the result is an extremely comfortable bed at every camp.

If the hiker is using a frame rucksack, the bedding is rolled into a bundle about five inches by eighteen inches, with the poncho on the outside. This bedroll is strapped on the top of the rucksack, perhaps under the flap which closes the main sack.

With the pack board, the other satisfactory pack for backpackers, both poncho and bedding are laid flat. The other contents of the pack are stacked atop them. Then everything is rolled into a bundle about fifteen inches by thirty inches with the poncho outside. If several short lengths of light rope or cord are used for binding this, these will come in handy for such camp uses as lashing together the pole framework for the lean-to.

COOKING AND EATING UTENSILS

Cooking utensils are the next consideration in the outfit. One must have appetizing, well-cooked, and nourishing food when doing strenuous work outdoors. This usually means for each meal something boiled in a kettle, a hot drink, and something cooked in a pan. For the lone camper, therefore, the minimum is two small kettles, always with covers and with bails by which they can be hung above a wood fire, a small frypan with folding handle, a tablespoon, and either an enamel or stainless steel cup.

The frypan will serve as a plate, and cereals can be eaten from the cup. One's pocket or sheath knife can be used for

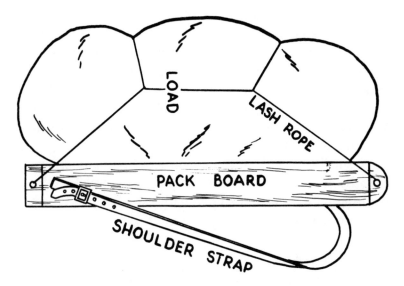

The contents of the pack are rolled into a bundle about fifteen inches by thirty inches, which is bound to the packboard with rope or cord.

food. A forked stick will do for a fork. One Hudson's Bay Company trader—a Scotsman—did surprisingly well with a couple of peeled green sticks, which he wielded like chopsticks!

Two nesting aluminum kettles, the larger holding a quart and a half and the smaller one a quart, together with an eight-inch aluminum frypan, are available from dealers in camping goods. Weighing twenty-five ounces, these take up no appreciable bulk in the pack, for grub and other essentials can be packed inside them.

When there are two or three persons in the party, this same outfit of two kettles and frypan will suffice, plus a light aluminum or stainless steel plate, stainless steel or enamel cup, and a spoon for each person. These utensils can be divided among the hikers.

For packing such articles as cereals, flour, and sugar, small plastic bags with tie strings can be used. If the plastic is transparent, the contents can be recognized at a glance. A small aluminum jar will do for items like butter and lard. Bacon may be wrapped in aluminum foil. Matches should be carried where they will be safe both from moisture and from the teeth of small animals such as squirrels.

A small dishcloth is a convenience. You can conserve soap by washing your dishes at the creek or lake edge, scouring with a bunch of grass with earth attached to the roots for scouring.

WHAT ELSE TO TAKE

Other desirable and essential additions to the camp outfit, depending to some degree on the individual and the country, may include: a small hand ax weighing, with sheath, a pound; the smallest toilet outfit you can get along with, containing perhaps a toothbrush, comb, hotel-size cake of soap, safety razor wrapped in a light towel, and mirror, together with any other necessities; a small medicine kit with usually just a cathartic, a few small adhesive bandages, some foot powder, several aspirin tablets, etc.; perhaps the smallest available flashlight, although this is not indispensable; writing materials, and a map of the locality.

Some extra clothing will be welcome but should be held to a minimum. After a strenuous day on the trail, the hiker is apt to arrive at his campsite pretty well damp with perspiration. A rubdown and the donning of dry underwear and socks will then pay off in refreshed well being. One set of light underwear and one extra pair of socks are therefore necessary for keeping a change freshly washed at all times.

One usually wears something such as a light khaki over-shirt when hiking in warm weather, while a medium-weight wool shirt will be desirable for wear after nightfall. In colder weather, a poplin or similar light jacket to go over the wool shirt will add warmth.

In his pockets each individual should have a filled, unbreakable, waterproof match case. He should also have a small luminous compass, a watch, a sturdy pocketknife, a handkerchief, sunglasses, if desired, and if he has to wear corrective spectacles, an extra pair of these.

One camera should suffice for a party, each hiker using it for such pictures as he wants. Ideal for backpackers are the light and compact 35-mm. jobs.

It is usually best for each hiker to carry his own shelter and bedding and to make his own individual camp each night. He then gets it exactly as he wishes, and he alone is responsible.

Now let us enumerate all this equipment in the form of a checklist, suggesting the weights of each article and the total weight of the basic pack.

Frame rucksack or pack board	3 lbs.	12 oz.
Plastic tarp and poncho	1 lb.	5 oz.
Down sleeping bag	3 lbs.	8 oz.
Cooking utensils*	1 lb.	12 oz.
Hand ax with sheath*	1 lb.	

*In a party of two or more, these articles will be used in common, each individual carrying his share. Add a plate, cup, and spoon to cooking utensils for each additional person.

Underwear and socks		12 oz.
Wool shirt, jacket, or sweater	1 lb.	8 oz.
Toilet articles		8 oz.
Flashlight, whetstone		6 oz.
Medicines, needles, thread, buttons		4 oz.

Total weight without food   15 lbs.

You can now figure on adding to the basic pack sufficient food to bring the total weight up to the maximum (as previously explained, twenty-five pounds for women and youths, or thirty-five pounds for men). About two and one-quarter pounds apiece per day will be eaten, indicating the number of days the grubstake will last without replenishment.

Many like to balance this in the following proportions by weight: starches 25 percent, sugars 15 percent, fats 10 percent, proteins 30 per cent, fruits 15 per cent, and beverages, seasoning (and matches) 5 percent.

Getting Ready for the Next Trip

Every outdoor trip is divided into three parts; the excitement of getting ready, the adventure itself, and finally the deep-down pleasure of reminiscence.

Although you may not plan to hit the trail again for a month or until next year, you will be missing one of the keenest joys of all if, as soon as one such excursion is over, you do not begin preparation for the next. You'll be passing up the pulse-quickening satisfaction of keeping your equipment ready, of purposefully thumbing catalogs and maps, and of scrawling terse reminders in a worn notebook carried for those moments when inspiration fires. Even in the midst of the steel bones and asphalt veins of the big city, this kind of preparation can keep you mighty close to those past days on the land and to those freer ones soon to come.

Then once again, almost before you know it, the wilderness night begins bulging from the west in a deep blue flood that drenches all but the last few waning embers of the sunset. Sweet black fumes lift from ready birch bark, and then the dry poplar with its clean medicinal odor catches hold. By you, in the forest's untroubled space, is everything you need: fishing gear, camping outfit, grub, gun, shelter, and friendly warmth. Life is very good.

5. Improvising Shelter in a Pinch

We camp out to get close to remote woods and waters that offer the best sport; to relish the fresh air, the freedom, and the good fellowship available nowhere else; and to get far enough away from the restraint, noise, and crowds of the big towns to enjoy the friendship of the seasons. If our camp is comfortable, so much the better. There is no reason why it should not be.

As the Hudson's Bay Company says after over three centuries in the farthest and most primitive reaches of this continent, "There is usually little object in traveling tough just for the sake of being tough."

Rough it, sure, if you want to prove to yourself that you *can* rough it. That's important to know; one day, anyone at all may be thrown entirely upon his own resources and forced to get along with a minimum of comforts. But roughing it is a developmental stage. Once we've successfully tested our ability to take it, a whole lot of doubts and inhibitions disappear. We find ourselves realizing that the real challenge lies in smoothing it. We come to appreciate that making it easy on ourselves takes a lot more experience and ingenuity than bulling it through the tough way.

A tent is not always a necessity for camping out. Shelter may often be better extemporized from materials we find in the woods.

When our forefathers came to the New World, the majority of them were from families that had been living in cities and towns or on farms for hundreds of years. Very few knew a thing about either camping or the woods.

When they went out hunting, exploring, or Indian fighting, they seldom took anything with which to shelter themselves. At night they simply lay down on the ground, perhaps under a tree, and tried to go to sleep. If it was cold and if danger was not too great, they lay close to a fire. If it rained, the chances were that they soon became soaked.

We think of them as hardy souls, able to rough it and to take it. As a matter of fact, nearly all had rheumatism as a result of exposure, and they usually died young. But they and their sons and daughters eventually learned from the Indians how to obtain shelter, warmth, and food in the wilderness.

If a fellow knocks around in the open long enough, the time comes sooner or later when he has to spend a night or more outdoors without any shelter except what nature can be persuaded to provide. Perhaps you have been hunting, fishing, or hiking; before you know it, twilight finds you far from base camp or human habitation. Perhaps you've become slightly turned around. You realize you cannot reasonably expect to get back to shelter before dark.

Whenever you find youself in this situation, the most sensible thing to do is to stop while a little daylight remains, make a bivouac, and lay up wherever you happen to be. There is nothing difficult or perilous about this. There are no wild animals in North America, with the exception of the grizzly and the polar bear, that are dangerous when unprovoked. At the very most you may miss a meal or two, or perhaps you may become a bit thirsty unless you happen to settle down near a spring or stream.

How to Avoid Needless Searching Parties

As far as your companions are concerned, a prior understanding may well have been agreed upon for the safety of all involved. Otherwise, you may feel obliged to press on, and they to get out unnecessarily and search. On sporting trips we have made with others back of beyond, there has always been a prior understanding that anyone should camp out any night he felt this advisable and, unless he signaled for help, no one should go out after him until at least noon of the next day.

No wilderness nights are more memorable, as a matter of fact, than one or two spent under these circumstances alone in the bush. In a wooded country whatever the weather, you can always manage to get a fair amount of slumber. If the approaching darkness promises to be warm and clear, simply select a dry and level spot for you bed, scrape slight hollows for shoulders and hips, cover the resting place with grass or pine needles or any soft dry forest litter, and then lie down and sleep the night out.

Often, however, the night is apt to be cold or at least cool, and there may be rain or snow. A campfire will then prove to be the most congenial of companions, affording both warmth and cheer.

Evergreen Bivouac

A big tree with thick foliage will ward off a lot of snow and rain. One of the easiest and best overnight niches can be quickly made by stripping off enough lower branches of a short thick evergreen tree to form a small cubbyhole. These branches, supplemented with more from other trees, can be used to make a soft dry flooring and to thatch the roof and sides.

An evergreen bivouac of this sort is so easily and rapidly fashioned that Brad and I have often made them so as to enjoy more fully the noon tea pail and not infrequently some sizzling kabobs and bannock as well. In any event, the tree chosen should first be shaken free of any snow or rain. If a storm has settled in heavily, a few pieces of birchbark or similar forest material will shed a lot of moisture.

If the dusk that is quickly dropping over the forest is bringing with it a deepening cold, try to select your bivouac site in a thick clump of small trees. If possible, let it be halfway down the lee slope of a hill, as this is the warmest spot in most country.

FIRE FOR WARMTH

During the daylight that is left, haul in all the dead and dry firewood you can find in the immediate locality. You may need a lot to last the night out. Include a few damp or rotting stumps and snags if possible, and perhaps a recently fallen big green limb or so; such branches will be handy for holding a more even heat and for retaining the fire.

If time is pressing, kindle your fire at nightfall and complete your preparations by its leaping illumination. Make everything as ready and comfortable as you reasonably can. If your clothes are damp, get them dry before trying to sleep. This you will probably be able to accomplish faster if you take most of them off and stretch and hang them on sticks not too close to flames or sparks.

Then put the heaviest and longest lasting wood on the

fire, arranging it so that the blaze will be at least as long as your body. Stretch out beside the dancing warmth. Relax and let the hoo-ho-ho-hoooooing of whisper-winged owls, the yipping of coyotes, and if you're very lucky, the sweet violent chorus of the timber wolves lull you to sleep.

In several hours or so, the coldness will awaken you. The fire has burned to embers. You grope carefully for the woodpile and toss some sticks into the coals. The pieces flare up quickly, flicking light across your bed and vitalizing it with fresh heat. You hunch up on an elbow, the living warmth of the blaze cheerful about you. We've both experienced this feeling you get—amid frozen beaver ponds in New Brunswick, or high by the Continental Divide when piñons made strange shapes against the desert moon, or in the velvet British Columbia night.

There is a wind high up in the trees, maybe, whirling splinters of ice from stars that shiver in a glacial blue-black sky. Some bird you've never heard before calls in the distance, like a moonbeam turned to sound. You lay back finally, all tension slackening. Almost at once it is morning, and you are ready to travel again. Put your fire dead out.

Lean-to

In colder weather, it is not enough merely to build a fire and stretch out beside it. Unless other provisions are made, such a blaze warms you in front, but those parts of your body facing away from the fire are so uncomfortably cold that restful sleep is impossible. Under such conditions, you need to consider ways of confining and reflecting the heat and of keeping the frosty breezes away.

One very easy solution is to arrange some sort of a

ridgepole about four feet off the ground, laying it perhaps between rocks or trees. Lean poles or sticks against this at such an angle that they reach the ground along the long back edge of your bed. You are, of course, going to make your fire so that it will warm the entire length of your body from feet to head.

On these poles, shingle or lay a quantity of spruce boughs, leafy branches, bark, or the like. You can even lean small evergreen trees in place, hooking alternate ones across the ridgepole so as to present a thick uniform wall against the night. The result, in any case, will be an open-faced camp with the fire built along the front of it. Shingle in the ends of your lean-to also, or pile a few small balsams or firs there, too.

Poles and boughs of pine or spruce are used to make a snug overnight shelter adequate for cold weather.

If you can kindle your fire against some reflecting surface, so much the better. The snugger you make your camp and the better the firewood you haul in, the longer will be your naps. There is no sense in being cold in a wooded country. Nothing is more enjoyable under favorable conditions than hobbling your cayuse and rolling up in the saddle blanket on star-silvered needles from nearby lodgepole pines. There are many other nights, however, when a half-hour occupied in readying a bivouac will be vastly repaid in convenience, ease, and refreshed well-being.

Other Shelters

There are no set rules governing siwashing. You do the best you can, as soon as you can, with the materials at hand.

Siwashing in an open tent affords one the opportunity of observing close at hand the creatures of the wild—such as these twin moose calves.

A shallow cave may be nearby where, heated by a fire in front, you can rest as easily as did your earliest ancestor who sought shelter in such a place.

Two or three boulders may be so grouped that, once a bough roof is thrown across them, they will afford snug sanctuary. A crude triangle stamped in deep snow, with the larger end floored and roofed with evergreen boughs and with the remaining corner reflecting a small fire, will provide warmth and shelter even if one is without bedding. The main precaution in the latter circumstance is to keep dry, as clothing which becomes damp or frozen loses its qualities of insulation in direct proportion to its wetness.

Based on joint experiences accumulated during many years in the wilderness, our reaction to closed-in tents is not particularly enthusiastic. These do have their uses, of course, especially during intense cold, in mosquito country under certain conditions, in construction and other work camps, and at public campgrounds where fires may be restricted and where privacy is certainly highly desirable.

Too often with such a shelter, however, you are needlessly shut up in a canvas shell that not infrequently is stuffy and poorly ventilated. You are closed in from the fresh air, the scenery, the delicious unspoiled odors, and the voices of the saucy chipmunks, birds, and other little dwellers of the wild places. We go camping largely to enjoy the congenial vigor of a wood fire, and, across its ever changing pattern, the contemplation of miles of beautiful country from the front of an open tent pitched on an attractive site. We are lulled by the unforgettable way wind sings through dislodged and disintegrating bark up near the timberline, and by the startling booming of live trees as freezing sap harmlessly bursts their innermost fibers. We're reassured somehow by the lap-lap-lap of tiny waves on the lake shore, the slap of a beaver's tail, the evening conversation of two loons, the whistling wings of ducks, and the leaping of what can be nothing less than the granddaddy of all trout. We yearn to be awakened many more nights by the hoarse exchange of bull and cow moose and by the way a solitary wolf lets its wavering voice lift and lower, rise and fall again, and then soar another time in three crescendos. All these you sense in a campfire tent.

CAMPFIRE TENT

This form of tent is very simple, consisting essentially of a canvas roof that is suspended and stretched from a ridgepole at an angle of about forty-five degrees. Large

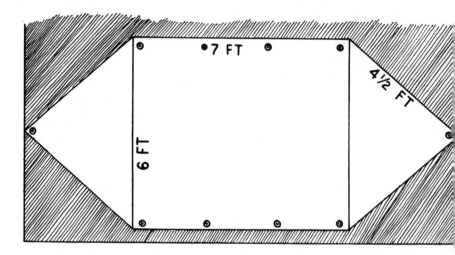

A tarp of light waterproof material or plastic sheeting makes the simplest one-man shelter when cut to the shape and dimensions above, and then suspended from a ridgepole.

enough to shelter the beds of two sleepers from rain or snow, it is entirely open at the front. The campfire is built from four to six feet in front of the peak of the roof, whose angle is such that it reflects both heat and light into the interior and down onto the beds.

The simplest form of campfire tent is merely a tarp—a rectangular sheet of canvas, light waterproof cotton, or plastic. The minimum effective size is about nine feet wide and fourteen feet long. Erected with the nine-foot length to the front and with the peak about seven feet above the ground, such a covering will shelter the beds of two campers who are sleeping with either their heads or feet to the front. It will allow, at the same time, about two and one-half feet of clearance above the ground at the inner ends of the beds.

Made of six-ounce waterproof cotton, such a tarpaulin will weigh about six pounds. Sewed of eight-ounce canvas, it will weigh closer to nine pounds. Plastic will weigh ounces. When pitched, it will be entirely open at the sides. If rain, wind, or snow blows in to a disagreeable extent, which seldom happens, the sides may be closed in by whatever way happens at the time to be most convenient. Heaping up a number of small evergreen trees, or any bushes with leafy tops, has proved adequate for us in bad weather ranging from blizzards to rainstorms of tropical intensity.

Such a simple tarpaulin is, as a matter of fact, about as good as any of the more elaborate lean-to tents. It is easy to put up. It is far less costly than more complicated structures. It is the most used of all shelters by the old-time woodsmen of the north, partly because cooking over the fire in front is easy except in an exceedingly heavy rain. Furthermore, a tarpaulin has a multitude of practical uses besides that of a shelter for sleeping.

THE BAKER TENT

The Baker form of tent, featured by most of our better tent makers is merely an elaboration of the already described tarpaulin arrangement. It has side walls in addition to the roof. There is a low wall at the rear of the roof. An awning attached to the peak can either be tied down to close the front completely, or it can be stretched out to form a canopy. The Baker is a fairly good tent for real wilderness. However, there are other ways, as we will consider in the next chapter, in which the same amount and bulk of canvas can be used to make a more effective and comfortable shelter.

6. Open Tents

The Spanish-American War instilled in me a strong desire for Army life. When I was mustered out of the service in the spring of 1900—a second lieutenant in the First Pennsylvania Infantry with $500 in my pocket—I learned there would be no opportunity to take an examination for entrance into the Army for a year. So I determined to have a grand hunting trip in the meantime. I'd been dreaming of such a hunt ever since getting my first rifle in 1891, a .22 Remington rolling block with which, the following year, I was fortunate enough to win my first rifle match for guides in the Adirondacks and to shoot my first deer unaided and alone.

So I gathered a small outfit. June found me in British Columbia, at the southern terminus of the Telegraph Trail to Alaska. There I bought three horses, rigging, and grub, and I started toward the top of the continent, not to return for nine glorious months.

Following the lessons derived from my boyhood experiences, the only shelter I had was a tarpaulin. Ten feet long and eight feet wide, this was made of light and closely woven cotton. I had sewed it myself, as a matter of fact, and had waterproofed it with paraffin.

The fifth day on the trail I ran into Bones Andrews, an old mountain man. We figured we might as well string along together for a few days. This association developed into a close friendship, and we agreed on a partnership to "hunt and prospect."

Bones had a dilapidated A-wall tent eight feet square. Not only was this full of holes, but it was heavy and difficult to erect. It wasn't long before we came to prefer my tarp, easily pitched as a lean-to. Bones finally traded his tent to some Chilkoot Indians for a ground hog robe (also known thereabouts as a marmot or whistler robe).

From then on—all through the warm summer and fall, and during the sometimes blustery winter—we used my tarp. We put it up at an angle of about forty-five degrees. We filled in the ends with boughs or small spruce trees whenever the weather was cold or stormy. Firewood was plentiful everywhere, just as it still is in that country, and we had a comfortable and cheerful camp even when temperatures dropped so low that Bones remarked that what we needed was a three-foot thermometer with zero at the top. We cooked, ate, worked, and just loafed in perfect ease.

In the years that followed I experimented extensively with shelter and camp equipment, partly because—as a result of such assignments as Director of Research and Development at Springfield Armory, Commanding Officer at Frankfort Arsenal, and Ordnance representative on the Infantry Board—experimentation in achieving greater performance became pretty much second nature with me.

One-Man Tents and Shelters

When a fellow camps by himself and does all his own work, there are certain features that he appreciates in a shelter. He wants a tent that is neither ponderous nor bulky. He likes something that is simple to erect.

The tent, furthermore, should be ruggedly capable of sheltering him from rain and snow. It should warm up quickly and easily from a wood fire in front, no matter what the direction of the wind. Also, it should be so arranged that moisture beating by the open front will not reach the bedding.

The immediate front of such a tent should provide a comfortable place in which to cook, repair equipment, oil rods and firearms, skin animals, and just plain lounge. Cooking in any weather short of a torrential downpour should be possible without getting wet. There should be convenient places to store the various classes of duffel, to dry clothing, and to hang a mosquito bar if desirable.

Such a tent should be laid out so that the camper will sleep lengthwise across the front, parallel to a long fire. His vital organs will thus be nearest the heart of the vitalizing heat. It will also be easy for him to get in and out of the sleeping bag. He will be able to see out of the tent while in bed, and hear also, and the genial warmth and light of the campfire will be at hand to be enjoyed and regulated if need be.

In very cold weather, a fire will not warm the back interior of any tent, but it always warms a tent of this sort for at least four feet back from the front. The habit, almost a religion among some, of sleeping with the feet toward the opening and the fire is all wrong. This places head and shoulders in the dark and poorly ventilated portion, makes it unnecessarily difficult to get in and out of bed, and pens one in needlessly. As a matter of fact, when we've been forced because of unexpected crowding to bunch up in a tent, both Brad and I—even during our greener years—automatically chose to sleep with head and shoulders toward embers and outdoors. During more than one night, we've been aroused by other occupants following suit.

It has often been said that if the feet are warm, the entire body will be comfortable. As a matter of fact, it is more important to have the vital organs near the center of the body warm; if they are, the whole body will indeed be at ease provided you don't turn in with wet socks.

With all these factors in mind, and after a lot of experience and experiment, I designed what I call a Hunter's Lean-to Tent. This I had made up by one of our leading tent makers, who marketed it as the Whelen Lean-to. I have used it in the North for twenty years, and so has Brad, and it is the best design we've ever found.

THE WHELEN LEAN-TO TENT

This design would not be satisfactory for a group of sportsmen with guides and cooks. For such a party I know of nothing that will equal a big tarp, twelve by fourteen feet or larger, pitched as a lean-to. But for one or two hunters, fishermen, or woods loafers who do their own work, including cooking, and who travel by pack train or canoe, shifting camp often, I know of no shelter so convenient and so comfortable. This holds true for any climate where firewood is plentiful—with the single exception of tropical mosquito country.

In principle, the Whelen Lean-to Tent is somewhat like the Baker Tent. It, too, has a steeply sloping shed roof. The side walls, instead of being perpendicular, splay outward and forward at the bottom. Their angle is such that the front end of each of those walls stakes down about two feet outward and two feet forward of where a perpendicular would reach the ground if dropped from an end of the six-foot tape ridge.

Thus, the walls slope at such an angle that they will reflect heat and light into the tent. They extend forward so as to keep winds and cold breezes from blowing around in front and chilling the little living sanctuary. With the walls spreading out in this way, a storage space is created at the head of the sleeping bag for personal effects, while another is provided at the foot for cooking utensils and grub.

The fact that there is no wall at the back of the roof simplifies both construction and pitching. It reduces cost. The low area beneath the roof at the rear can be utilized for stowing duffel not in use.

Loops are attached to the tape ridge through which the ridgepole is thrust. On the underside of this six-foot tape ridge are two other loops which will support a short pole on which clothing may be hung either to be out of the way or to dry.

A thirty-inch-wide awning is sewed to the ridge. This can either be thrown back over the ridgepole or extended out to prolong the roof. In case of storm, for example, the awning is stretched out forward and downward from the ridge so that it shelters the ground in front, keeps moisture from driving into the tent, and creates a dry space in which to sit and cook over the fire.

To extend the awning in this fashion, you don't have to use bothersome guy ropes. You simply cut a pair of poles about six feet long and sharpen both ends. Stick one end of each pole in the large grommet at each outer corner of the awning. Plant the other ends at the foot and at the head of the sleeping bag. The weight of these will keep the awning extended and taut without any guy lines being in the way to snag you or trip you. The front edge of the awning will then be about four feet above the ground where heat and light from the fire can still come in under it.

To pitch this tent, cut a ridgepole about ten feet long. Thread this through the loops of the tape ridge. Support the pole by trees or shear poles, as suggested by the illustrations, about six feet above the ground. Then stake down the back and sides, and your tent is ready for occupancy.

The tent shown is one-man size. It will comfortably accommodate two campers, sleeping side by side parallel to the front. The man whose turn it is to build the fire in the

In the Whelen Lean-to Tent, a ten-foot ridgepole is supported by trees or shear poles about six feet above the ground.

morning snoozes on the outside. He then can lean out of his bag, place shavings and split wood in the fireplace, touch a match to them, and get up ten minutes later in the reflected warmth.

Made of Aberlite or Green Waterproof Egyptian cotton running approximately six ounces per square yard, the Whelen Lean-to Tent weighs about seven pounds. It is also available in an extralight long-stapled cotton weighing five pounds. It is seven feet deep, six feet wide at the rear, and about ten feet wide in front. This front can become the coziest and warmest living room easily available in the farther places. The sides somehow do much to keep smoke from blowing into the tent and, in fact, eradicate this nuisance entirely if you have a tier of back logs a foot high behind the campfire.

The Whelen Lean-to Tent is not adapted to temperatures of twenty degrees below zero and colder, for it would then take too many hours of ax work to bring in the firewood necessary for heat and for cooking. When such frigidity endures for any considerable time, you need a closed tent with a stove. Besides an ax, you should then also have either a bucksaw or a swede saw to cut the wood into the short lengths necessary to feed the firebox.

THE FORESTER TENT

If your problem is to cut weight or costs, the Forester Tent is a good solution. It is one of the best tents ever devised for a chronic woods loafer, particularly for one who wishes to live close to nature and who objects to spending any of his outdoor hours confined in a closed canvas cell.

The Forester Tent is the cheapest of all tents either to buy or to make yourself. It is the easiest and quickest to pitch. Considering its weight and bulk, it is the most comfortable in which to live and do your few camp chores. With the exception of the Whelen Lean-to Tent, it is the easiest to warm with a campfire in front.

A little Forester Tent has gone with me, too, on many of my trips into the Far North. It has often been used there by my companions while I was sleeping in my Lean-to Tent. The two shelters pitched ten feet apart facing each other, with a fire flickering between, make about the most comfortable camp imaginable.

"Most men are needlessly poor all of their lives because they think they must have such a house as their neighbors have," an old woodsman said more than a century ago. "Consider how slight a shelter is absolutely necessary."

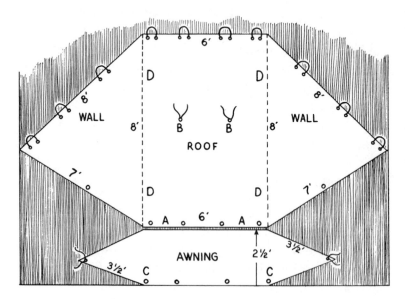

Pattern for making the Whelen Lean-to Tent.

Bugproofing Tent Interiors

There are times and places where mosquitoes, black flies, and other winged biters can take much of the immediate pleasure out of life unless we are ready for them. Especially in the Far North during the long days when dusk blends imperceptibly with dawn, mosquitoes are often to be encountered in air-darkening clouds that are absolutely unbelievable to people from farther south.

PATTERN FOR MAKING WHELEN LEAN-TO TENT

For one or two campers, sleeping with their sides to the front. Make of closely woven waterproof cotton about five to seven ounces per square yard, and cut and sew to the shape and dimensions shown, allowing one inch around the edges for hemming.

A. Tape ridge with outside loops for ridgepole, and two loops on underside for clothing pole.

B. Loops or cords sewed to outside of roof, in which to insert poles when necessary to remove "belly" from roof in snow or heavy rain.

C. Large grommets, one inch in diameter, in which to insert sharpened poles which keep awning extended to the front when desired.

D. Loops sewed inside at junction of roof and walls from which to hang mosquito bar when needed.

PATTERN FOR MAKING FORESTER TENT

For one or two campers, with beds arranged along side walls.

Make of closely woven waterproof cotton about five to seven ounces per square yard, and cut and sew to the shape and dimensions shown, allowing one inch all around the edges for hemming. Note how bottoms of sides set back one foot to make tent sit right on ground. To manage this, cut pattern from rectangular canvas as shown by dotted lines, then angle the front and back. The rear wall is cut off square at top, and when this is sewed to the main body of the tent at the rear it leaves a hole at the top of the rear wall through which the ridgepole is stuck. Total weight: four to five pounds.

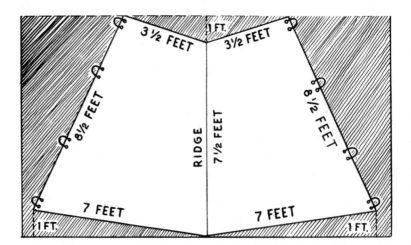

Pattern for making the Forester Tent.

A great deal has been done to lick these scourges since the building of the Alaska Highway and the activity in Alaska dating from the Second World War. A lot of people who could do something about it learned at first hand in those practical laboratories that mosquitoes can be a lot tougher obstacle than even the sub-Arctic's incomparable mud and muskegs.

There are several easy ways in which the camper may combat these pests. One, or in extreme cases a combination of all, is sure to be so successful that no one need longer dread the critters.

Tents may be protected by screened doors and windows in addition to sod cloths or sewed-in floors. Individual mosquito bars are, along this same line of defense, very effective. Annoyers that still manage to get inside enclosures can be killed or immobilized by insecticides that to some extent will discourage them in the first place. Exposed portions of the body may be kept so coated with harmless and not unpleasant repellents that usually no insect will land on the skin for more than an instant. Biteproof clothing, extending even to gloves and headnets in drastic cases, may be worn.

The subject is, as we both can testify from long and considerable personal experience, a broad and important one. It is covered at length later.

7. Stoves for Tents and Shelters

For camps in the wilderness where wood is available, we both ordinarily prefer the open blaze in conjunction with some sort of a lean-to shelter.

Such a campfire takes a part of anyone back to when our earliest ancestor cooked his meat for the first time and, rolled in furs, spent his initial night in a shallow cave warmed by the newly harnessed flicker of flame. It is the atavistic memory of this discovery, that lifted men above the animals, which is one of the chief urges that draws a lot of us back again and again into the wilderness. A camp without a wood fire, in fact, seems to be no camp at all.

Senses neglected in the humdrum of city life expand to an exquisite sensitivity under the influences of an honest campfire. The friendly deliciousness of smoke, some of which probably still perfumes your outdoor clothing from the last adventure, seeks you out as you get the camp in order. Then there's the special outdoor allure not available in the costliest restaurants that hardwood embers—with maybe a slight seasoning of pine—impart to food roasted, broiled, or baked over them.

The campfire cheerfully shows its superiority, too, when

it comes to toasting yourself or drying your wet clothes. Such a fire costs nothing, and the wood that you have the satisfaction of gathering for it enjoys the added virtue of warming you twice.

The gasoline type of stove is ideal, and often a must for many public camping grounds. It is good for the places where firewood is no longer to be had and where even space may be limited. It is inexpensive, easily and compactly packed, and durable. It can be used atop a handy metal stand that supports it at normal stove height and, when not in use, folds into a small bundle that is easily stowed in the car or boat.

Primus Stove

The one-burner primus stove has a unique record among explorers, campers, and outdoorsmen. For the past eighty years it has been used by all Arctic and Antarctic exploring expeditions, as well as by at least 90 percent of all Alpine climbers. If you are contemplating a trip into some such area as the rich Barren Lands—before which the treeline abruptly ends, not dwindling away gradually as might be expected—a compact primus stove weighing little more than a pound will be a good thing to take along.

These efficient little heaters may be obtained in units burning alcohol, kerosene, gasoline, naphtha, benzine, and other liquid fuels. A two-and-one-half-pound outfit with less than six inches of height and diameter may be secured that includes, in addition to the small brass stove, two nesting pots and two frypans as well as a shield against the winds that blow across treeless terrain. There is also a twenty-four-ounce outfit nesting three and one-half inches and seven inches in diameter, that includes stove, two pots, potholder, windshields, and a combination lid and pan.

Wood-Burning Stoves

Whenever a stove is to be packed into territory where firewood is available, a sheet-metal, wood-burning model has decided advantages. You'll seldom see one today in city stores, and they're unfamiliar to campers with little experience. But along the receding frontiers in whose forests you still encounter old-timers, these wood-burning models usually are the only portable stoves ever considered.

Such a stove usually weighs a little more than the gasoline stove and, although available in folding models, is generally bulkier. But there is no fuel to transport, and the folding sheet-metal stove is not difficult to carry even over a portage or on a packhorse.

You can cook on such a stove in the rain. With a little care, it will safely warm closed tents as well as log shacks. Many sourdoughs we know, as a matter of fact, have no other stove even in their home cabins. It is easy to dry clothing around it. Broiling and toasting over an open pot hole can be a comparative pleasure.

A woodstove is particularly handy for river trips in the large kicker-propelled boats that travel the broad and often sluggish streams at the roof of this continent. There, odds and ends of driftwood quickly afford concentrated heat, protected from the ravenous winds often howling along such shores. By providing a shallow box filled with sand or some other such base, you can even cook enroute.

If the stove you select has an oven, and there is usually no good reason why it should not, baking and roasting will be possible. If it is without an oven, a folding reflector baker can be used.

Some sourdoughs, particularly in cabins, utilize a drum oven. This is a small metal compartment which is set in the stovepipe. There, for cooking and heating purposes, it utilizes warmth that would otherwise escape up the smoke outlet.

The standard A-Wall tent is best adapted to a wood-burning stove. Such a tent seven by nine feet is about the smallest that is suitable for this. A nine-by-twelve size is better for two men because the beds will then not be too near the heat.

The stove should not be closer than eighteen inches to any part of the fabric. The tent should not have a sewed-in floor, although you can get around this by using insulation such as an asbestos mat or a container filled with sand or loam. Using rocks alone is not wise, for dangerous sparks can slip unnoticed among them.

If the stove has no legs and you would like to raise it to a more convenient height, just drive four stout stakes into the ground and cap each with an old tin can. Of course, the stove can be set on flat rocks, too. In cabins, a pole enclosure about a foot wider all around than the stove, and generally about a foot high, is often built and filled with rock and loam to provide a base. You see wood-burning stoves, propped up on four tin cans in cabins as well.

Such stoves are provided with adjustable drafts. If necessary, an additional damper can easily be inserted in the pipe. You can thereby regulate the heat to a large extent. But you should never fill a stove of this sort full of wood and then go away and leave it with the drafts open. If you do, it is apt to become red-hot in a hurry, and then you may have the stage set for a conflagration.

With carefully selected wood, it is often possible to build a fire that will last for four or five hours. If an all-night fire is desired, someone generally has to get up during the small hours to stoke it up. A lot of prospectors and trappers live comfortably the whole winter in the frigid North in A-Wall tents with small sheet-metal stoves. Always maintain ventilation as a guard against carbon monoxide poisoning.

STOVEPIPE HOLE

The telescoping stovepipe had best go straight up through the roof of the tent. Less effective and more hazardous is the practice of angling the pipe through the back wall by the use of two elbows. The outlet should, in any event, extend at least six inches above the peak of the tent. This will not only ensure better draft, but it will also reduce the danger of sparks being blown directly against the canvas. It is often a good idea to top this pipe with an inexpensive spark arrester, particularly if you are using softwoods or camping in thick dry woods.

There should be a fire guard where the pipe goes through the tent cloth. Consisting of an opening centered in some fireproof material which replaces a small section cut from the fabric, this may be obtained from large outfitters as well as from most tent makers. A wire-reinforced asbestos guard is better than a metal one because, in addition to being reasonably flexible and more durable, it will not set up a disconcerting rattle on breezy days.

This collar may be obtained with flaps that will cover the opening when a stovepipe is not angling up through it. You can also leave the original tent fabric attached at the top so that it can be rolled up out of the way and tied or snapped across the opening.

Sheepherder Stove

The most famous as well as one of the better stoves for tents and other small shelters is the Sheepherder Stove of the West. This is a rather large article of the box type, with sufficient capacity for cooking a meal for five or six campers. It is about twenty-seven inches long, a foot high and wide, and has a rapidly heating oven five by eight by eleven inches. It weighs twenty-seven pounds.

Any stove of sheet iron or sheet steel will burn out in time, but the Sheepherder has the reputation of lasting longer than any other stove made of such materials. The one used on my last winter trip had been providing almost continuous service for four years.

The only place I know of where you can get the Sheepherder Stove is from Chet Rice at the Smilie Company, 575 Howard Street, San Francisco, California. These large camp outfitters also have a smaller and lighter stove, twenty by twelve by twelve inches. Including a small oven, this weighs only a dozen pounds. Less expensive, it is adequate for two or three campers. It does not have the longevity of the Sheepherder, however. Both varieties come with telescoping pipe.

There is also a still-available model made by Sims Stoves of Lovell, Wyoming. It folds flat to a thickness of three inches, and it has a stovepipe. This is a splendid, well-made little stove. Because it is so easy to pack, I believe I would prefer it to the Sheepherder for use with a reflector baker if I had to carry it on a horse.

8. The Campfire

What remains most fondly in our minds after a wilderness trip, I suppose, is the campfires: the warm blaze that takes the kinks out of you in the misty morning; the handful of crackling twigs that boils the kettle at noon; the cooking coals at the end of the day's sport when the odors make your mouth water for that fresh liver or those flaky rainbows; the cheerful flames behind whose sanctuary you sit while the darkening forest comes to life.

There is also the long night fire beside which you lie secure, obedient to no needs but those imposed by darkness, cold, and vagrant wind, and to no mortal's laws but your own. The campfire then seems little more than a pinprick in an infinity.

Much of the success of a camping trip, as well as a great deal of the pleasure, is going to depend on your having the right kinds of fires. This does not mean, certainly, that campfires should be built in just one way. It all depends upon where you are, what you have, and whether your most pressing needs at the moment are for warmth, light, or nourishment.

The principles governing outdoor fires do not change,

however. In the realm of camping there is probably no one set of essentials so often mismanaged. A poor fire can cause a multitude of troubles. A good one is a joy to all around it.

Safety

It does not pay to take chances with fire. Never kindle one on flammable ground such as that made up largely of decomposed and living vegetation. Fire will sometimes eat down deep in such footing. An individual may think he has put his fire out but often it may not be entirely extinct. Unseen and unsuspected, it may smolder for days and weeks underground. It may lie nearly dormant during an entire winter. With the warmth and increasing dryness of spring, it may regain new vigor until one hot day a strong wind may cause it to bloom into a growling, exploding, devastating forest fire.

When you leave a camp or bivouac in a potentially dangerous area for more than a few minutes, put out that fire. Saturate it with water. Stir up the ground beneath and around it, working and soaking ashes and dust into mud. Dig around it until you are certain no root or humus will lead the blaze away like a fuse. Feel with your hands to make sure that all heat has been safely diminished. Examine the vicinity for any activity resulting from sparks and flying embers.

In some country, particular precaution must be taken when a Dutch oven is used. In a few areas, especially during dry seasons, this shallow kettle with its rimmed cover should not be used at all except when you remain on the spot. Make sure, in any event, wherever fire can be a menace, that the oven is buried in mineral soil and that no combustible material of any sort, be it roots or decaying forest litter, is near enough to be started smoldering.

Kindling

A woodsman is known by the time it takes him to build his fire with whatever wilderness materials there may be at hand. If birch grows in your locality, the very best kindling is birchbark. Enough shreds of this can be pulled off by hand so that ordinarily there is no need, even deep in the bush, to disfigure the tree.

In evergreen country you need never have difficulty in starting a blaze in any kind of weather. A fairly tight handful of the dead resinous twigs that abound in the lower parts of all conifers will burst readily into flame at the touch of a match. The only exception you'll occasionally run across occurs in damp cold weather. Then, freezing moisture sometimes forms light sheaths of ice over the forest. When this happens, the solution still remains simple: you have only to expose the dry oily interiors of the dead branches.

Shavings from pitch pine light very easily. So do shavings from any dead wood you find adhering to standing evergreens. If no softwood is about, look for dead wood on other trees. If you do have to use fallen litter for kindling, be sure that what you choose is firm and dry.

Fuzzsticks, when you need to bother with them, start a fire quickly. They are made by shaving down on a piece of wood again and again, not detaching the curls. These are commonly employed instead of paper, incidentally, to start stove fires in the backwoods. Light these fuzzsticks, and all other kindling, so that the flames will be able to eat upward into the fresh fuel.

Ordinarily, dry materials are best to get the fire going. The job can also be done with live birch and live white ash, however, by splitting out kindling and making fuzzsticks.

Starting the Campfire

An easy way to go about building a campfire throughout much of this continent is first to get a few scraps of something exceedingly flammable. This may be a few wisps of birchbark. Pile loosely over the shreds of bark something a trifle less combustible, such as small, dry evergreen twigs.

Above this nucleus lean a few larger seasoned conifer stubs. Also in wigwam fashion, so that ample oxygen will reach all parts of the heap, lay up some dead hardwood. Then ignite the birchbark so that the flames will eat into the heart of the pile.

The lighting should almost always be accomplished with a single match. Even on those occasions when plenty of matches are at hand, the thus slowly acquired skill may on some later day mean the difference between a warmly comfortable camp and a chilly and miserably damp one.

Long wooden matches are best. These must be held so that any draft reaching them will feed the fire down the wooden stem where it will be able to keep burning. This you will accomplish in whatever way seems best at the moment. You may face the wind with your two hands cupped in front of the flaming match. You may stretch out between the breeze and carefully heaped flammables so that your body will act as a shield. You may use your jacket or any other handy articles, such as large sheets of bark, to protect the first feeble flames.

In any wooded area, a campfire can always be thus built

from materials at hand. You can either find or make a sheltered nook. Even when a cold rain is freezing as it falls, shavings and kindling can be provided with a knife. If you don't have a knife, you can still shatter and splinter enough dead wood with which to kindle a blaze. If birchbark is available, one sheet will form a dry base on which to arrange campfire makings, while other bark angled about and above these will keep off moisture until the fire is crackling.

How to Keep Matches Dry and Handy

It is well to keep a waterproof container filled with wooden matches whenever you are in the bush. This should be unbreakable so that even should you happen to slip in a stream, the matches will remain intact. This match case, which may well include some provision whereby it can be attached to the person or clothing, should be stowed where it will not be lost. In the North, we figure it is inexpensive insurance to carry a second filled container. Other matches may be conveniently distributed among the pockets where they will be readily available for ordinary uses.

B'iling the Kittle

The Northern woodsman, particularly the Canadian, must sip his steaming cup of tea at noon and contemplate its rapidly changing surface colors even if he has nothing to eat. This is almost a religion up under the Aurora Borealis and is called "b'iling the kittle." For the temporary fire required, nothing elaborate is needed. Sufficient is a handful of dry wood that will flare up briefly and as quickly disintegrate to ashes, a few gray feathers of which invariably swirl up to float almost unnoticed in the dark brew.

The Camp Fire Club of America for years has sponsored an annual competition in boiling a kettle of water, with prizes and with time limits for qualification. The participant is given a billet of dry wood about five by twelve inches, a sharp hand ax, a kettle holding about two quarts of water, and one match. That is all.

The best technique is first to split the wood to include three full-length pieces about three-fourths of an inch thick. These three sticks are driven into the ground to form a triangle about six inches high upon which the kettle is set. The remainder of the wood is reduced to shavings and split kindling which are placed under the kettle and ignited. If the competitor is experienced, he has picked up a small dry pebble on which to strike his match, and he kneels facing the wind. I know of no quicker way to boil tea water than this.

The woodsman is not so elaborate. He builds a fire in the easiest way he can, depending on what fuel there is at hand. He cuts a green pole several feet long. This tea stick he shoves into the ground so that one end extends over the center of the heat. He may adjust its height by propping the stick up with a rock or chunk of wood.

The kettle he hangs by its bail at the end of the tea stick. This container, incidentally, is very often a large tin can near whose rim opposite holes have been punched and a handle, perhaps a foot of light copper or snare wire, has been inserted.

Cooking Fires

If in addition to heating water for tea, you want to fry some steaks and maybe boil up some nearby wild onions,

"B'iling the kittle" for tea is a noontime ritual.

one handy method that will do away with a lot of teetering and tipping is to dig or stamp a trench in the ground. This may be about six inches across, six inches deep, and eighteen inches long. Place this trench lengthwise to the wind to assure a good draft, and in it build your fire. Kettle, skillet, and other utensils can then be steadied across it.

The fire must have oxygen with which to burn, of course. If the kindling and other wood is packed too compactly, the result will be a smudge that will soon smoke out. You can sometimes help the blaze along by blowing on the flames or by fanning them. If the day is unusually quiet and the fuel none too ardent, however, you will do better to build the ordinary sort of above-ground cooking fire.

THE LONG COOKING FIRE

We like to have all the makings of our meals—hot meat, vegetables, biscuits, and beverage—served at once. This means that for dinner several receptacles and perhaps a reflector baker will be functioning all at once, with probably one cook to manage everything. A job of this sort is hard to control if you are using the ordinary round fire. More functional is a fire about eight inches wide and four or five feet long.

A cooking fire of this sort can be built between two fairly dry logs some four to six inches in diameter. Let these be about five feet long. If they are raised an inch or so by stones or billets of wood, air will be able to circulate freely beneath them. Build you fire of long wood placed between these two logs. Keep adding fuel, preferably split hardwood, and let it burn down until you have either a bed of coals or an enduring fire that does not blaze up over a foot high. It will then be ready for the vittles.

In the meantime, cut two posts of green wood about two inches in diameter, each with a fork at the top. Drive these into the ground at either end of your two logs so that a green crosspiece laid between the crotches will extend above the center of the fire. Make pothooks for each kettle as shown in the sketch.

If you are using a reflector baker, set it on the ground about a foot from the fire. While baking, encourage a high blaze in front of it with split kindling.

Grates and Irons

A substantial wire grid, available from dealers in camp equipment, will provide a convenient base on which to set pots and pans above a wood fire and over which to broil meat. Some of these have folding legs which, stuck into the forest floor, will hold kettles and frypan the desirable eight inches or so above the ground.

Our own experience deep in the bush, however, has been that these sharp extremities are somewhat of a menace when one is constantly on the move. We have removed them, partly also to save weight. The grids can as handily be laid across rocks or billets of wood. In a stony spot, this has to be done anyway.

A similar arrangement, less bulky to pack, is two iron rods about one-half inch in diameter and four feet long, or flats or angle irons of similar stiffness. Support them above your fire with rocks or logs at each end, and have them just far enough apart so the smallest kettle will not slip down between.

Keeping Fire Makings Ready

Before you turn in at night and certainly before you leave camp, even if only for the day, provide a plentiful supply of fuel with which the next fire can be built. These makings may include birchbark, three of four good fuzzsticks, some split kindling, and a few pieces of larger wood. Place all these under cover where they will be sure to keep dry.

You may arrive back in camp dog-tired, cold, and wet, with numb hands that will scarcely grasp a knife for whittling. Or when your turn comes to build the morning fire, it may be raining or snowing. It won't take many such experiences to make you remember to have the makings always ready.

One of the unforgivable sins of the North Woods is to quit a camp or cabin without leaving both kindling and a plentiful supply of dry firewood by the stove or fireplace.

Night Fire

Suppose you have a cooking fire built in front of your lean-to tent, and the weather is either nippy or downright cold. When the evening meal is over, take away the pot-hooks and poles. Drive a couple of posts about ten inches behind the backlog of your present fire, slanting them a little backwards. Pile up a wall of good stout logs, dry or green, against these. Over your cooking fire lay some smaller logs. Pretty soon you'll have quite a blaze, with the log wall in the rear reflecting the heat back into your tent—a cheerful fire before which to spend a frosty night.

If you will build up this fire just before turning in, you may be able to keep it going all night. It will then provide warmth while you sleep and, in the morning, a bed of coals that will do for cooking breakfast. There is no sure formula, however, for keeping a campfire alive all night without attention. Sometimes it will hold, but if the heat is necessary for comfortable sleeping, more often someone has to pile out around 2:00 A.M. to freshen it.

This is not much of a chore to an old woodsman. He lays on some logs that have already been cut, and perhaps he lights a stub of a pipe from a coal. Never does smoke smell so sweet. An owl hoots. The sparks and the smoke go straight up to heaven where gleams Orion's belted brightness. It's good to be awake at such a time.

9. Bedding for the Outdoors

No sleeping bag or blanket of itself produces any warmth. In the absence of a fire, the human body is ordinarily the only stable heat-generating source in a wilderness camp.

The average man, sleeping or lounging relaxed beside a campfire, liberates somewhat less than a hundred calories of heat every hour. This output can be increased in two ways. Rigorous exertion can, over the day, multiply the yield as much as six times. Even shivering, a form of muscular exercise and one of nature's safeguards against freezing, will build up the release of body warmth several times. Eating, too, stimulates the caloric output. The increase is quicker although of shorter duration with carbohydrates, greater and more lasting with proteins.

When exposed to cold, the skin automatically begins to shut off surface blood circulation. It can thus decrease the heat loss from the skin by as much as a fourth. Alcohol, it so happens, prevents this natural thermostat from functioning properly, bringing on rapid and sometimes dangerous heat losses at the same time that the individual may be deluded into believing himself warmed and stimulated. Wind, as well as low temperature, produces chilling and accelerated dissipation of bodily warmth.

All that a sleeping bag or any other bedding can do, therefore, is to delay the loss of body warmth by insulating the individual both against undue waste of that heat and against encroachments of cold and wind.

The most effective insulation known for this purpose is dry, still air. Thus the effectiveness of bed materials in keeping one warm is in direct proportion not to their weight but in the number of dead air cells they contain. The thicker a sleeping robe or blanket is and the fluffier its nature, the more inert air it affords.

Two Ways to Make a Fur Blanket

Indians of the more remote North often made blankets of rabbit skins and similar furs. They still do, for that matter, although the squaws' activities along these lines have decreased considerably; tribes have found it easier to come by money and buy commercial blankets and sleeping bags. The job of making a fur blanket is not a difficult one, however. Anyone on hand during a rabbit year can fashion such a robe. There are two general methods.

One way is to stretch and dry the skins of varying hares, snowshoe rabbits, marmots, or similar small creatures whose light and fragile pelts are not particularly valuable. Each skin is then cut in a long ribbon about three-fourths of an inch wide. This is done by starting outside and cutting around the circumference. A ribbon several yards long is thus obtained from the larger pelts.

The ribbon is then spiraled around a rawhide cord, often known locally as babiche, whose manufacture is illustrated

Cutting babiche, the rawhide thongs and laces used to fashion a fur blanket.

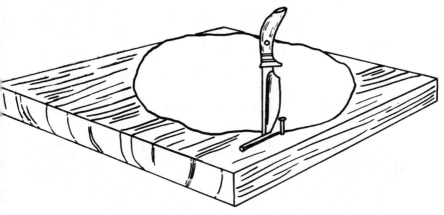

here. The resulting fur ropes are sewed together at the ends, making a single long line. A pole frame the size of the desired blanket is lashed or otherwise fastened together. The fur rope is woven into it to form the blanket, which is finally bound on the edges with cloth or buckskin.

The weave customarily is very loose. You can poke a finger through it anywhere. A blanket about five by seven feet, therefore, weighs in this stage little more than a pound. These fur robes have never been very durable, and the hair keeps coming out. To offset both these faults to some extent, they're often quilted between two thicknesses of some fabric such as light wool blanket.

The second method consists of shingling a blanket or other fabric with tanned whole hides lapped an inch or so. The basted pelts are then sandwiched protectively by sewing over them another piece of jute, canvas, blanket, or any other hardy fabric.

Sleeping Bag Fillers

Fifty years ago sleeping bags consisted of several thicknesses of wool blankets sewed into bag form inside an outer sack of canvas. They were, in fact, just a more or less convenient and controversial way of preventing the kicking off of blankets during sleep. Horace Kephart, calling them unpleasant traps, did not disagree that on the whole sleeping

The pelts of varying hares, snowshoe rabbits, marmots, or similar small creatures are too light and fragile to be particularly valuable, but their skins can be made into fur blankets.

bags were an accursed invention of a misguided soul.

The better modern sleeping bags utilize more effective insulating materials which are at once thicker and lighter than blankets, affording therefore much more dead air space pound for pound. The best insulating filler, providing maximum warmth with minimum weight, is white goose down.

Next in thermal value come some of the new synthetic materials such as dacron: these are light and durable as well as impervious to mold, moths, and mildew. Dacron has a heat-retaining capacity about midway between goose down and wool. If weight and bulk are not primary considerations, dacron is desirable as a filler for ordinary summer and fall use because of its low cost as compared to down. It is not as good as pure waterfowl down for backpacking or for extreme cold.

Not very much money should be spent for a bag with a questionable or mediocre filler such as feathers. It would be more prudent to wait and come up with a few more dollars to purchase one of the less expensive synthetic bags, getting along with blankets in the meantime if necessary.

How to Keep Warm in a Sleeping Bag

Down sleeping robes weighing three pounds are usually satisfactory when temperatures are above zero. For fall hunting in the North and at high altitudes, five-pound down bags will provide comfortable repose in cold as low as ten to twenty degrees below zero.

We've both put in good nights in our eiderdowns when the colored alcohol in the thermometer has contracted more than 100 degrees below freezing. When it's that icy, you appreciate five to six pounds of down in addition to a shaggy woolen lining that doesn't let you shiver too long when you pile in and draw the top up over your head. Inside the bag is the place for your head to be when the sap in the trees starts freezing, and the banging and snapping of tearing, bursting fibers joins the heavier connonade of expanding ice. Your nose, however, must be outside, both for fresh air and to avoid filling the bag with moist vapor.

On the frostiest nights with too light a bag, you may have to turn in with your clothes on. These should be absolutely dry. Loosen all tight areas beforehand and empty your pockets, placing the contents where none will be lost. If you have a flashlight which you may have cause to use during the darkness, take it in the bag with you. Otherwise, extreme cold may immobilize the batteries.

When possible, it will be better to figure on carrying a heavier bag and sleeping in it raw. Flannel pajamas are ordinarily appreciated, but in very cold weather you'll actually be more comfortable without them because they will retain a certain amount of body moisture.

Except for something to protect the feet, you won't need to don anything if you have to haul out for any reason. The body will retain its own aura of warmth for a couple of minutes or so. Such exposure will not be harmful in any respect or even unpleasant. You'll probably be shivering when you crawl back into the sack, but warmth will soon take over and almost at once you'll be drowsing again.

It is best to choose a sleeping robe suitable for the lowest temperatures you expect to encounter. A good down robe that will keep you warm on nights when twinkling ice crystals form a scintillating ceiling close above the throbbing earth will still be pleasant during the warmth of summer.

By that time you will be using it nearly open and you will probably be sleeping with at least your head, arms, and chest uncovered. A robe with snaps—preferable to the vulnerable zipper for wilderness use—can be adjusted most satisfactorily to changing temperatures.

Protecting the Heat-Retaining Qualities of Sleeping Bags

The warmth of a down bag, and to a lesser extent that of all bags, can be regulated to a very large degree by the frequency with which it is aired. In very cold weather, daily airings will keep the down fluffed out and will expel the heat-conducting moisture. In hot weather you'll find the bag more comfortable if it is aired only as it lies. Care should be taken when the robe is hung across a line to suspend it parallel to the tubes that contain the insulation.

One difficulty experienced with sleeping robes in which down and similar fillers are used is that this insulation has a tendency to shift toward the bottom. This leaves the upper area of the robe vulnerable to low temperatures. In many instances, this slippage results in the expense and nuisance of returning the article to the factory for renovation.

But you can redistribute the filler yourself on the spot, as a matter of fact. The process is very simple. Open the robe. Lay it on a hard surface, such as the ground or floor, with the inside upward. Procure a supple stick about a yard long. Then start beating the robe slightly from the foot up toward the center. You will be able to feel when a reasonably uniform thickness has been returned. If necessary, turn the robe over and go through the same process on the other side.

Mummy Bags

Outfitters supply small, body-fitting mummy bags which contain from two to three pounds of down and which roll into very small bundles weighing about twice the weight of the filler. Such bags are intended chiefly for hikers and climbers who have to pack all their equipment on their backs. They offer wonderful possibilities in putting together a go-light outfit. One of us has ridden many wilderness miles with a little bag of this sort, still as good as new after ten years of rough usage, rolled in a small tarpaulin in along with some grub and other essentials and tied behind the saddle.

Experienced mountain climbers have found the mummy bag to be satisfactory down to about ten degrees above freezing provided it is used in a small Alpine tent with some sort of soft insulation under it. If the temperature gets too cold for a night or so, you can turn in fully clad, except for boots, in dry and preferably fresh clothing.

These mountain bags, which can be bought to fit your height are made about eighteen inches wide at the bottom and up to some thirty-six inches wide at the top. The user is thus encased like a mummy. When he turns over during sleep the entire bag is apt to turn over with him. This is not objectionable after one becomes accustomed to it. As a matter of fact, after a few nights you can get in the habit of holding the top down with your two hands and maneuvering sufficiently with the hips and feet to keep the bag in place when you move. This soon comes to be second nature. Vena Angier, for example, prefers this model of eiderdown.

Some folks, however, never do feel fully relaxed in the mummy bag, particularly if they have slept many months in a large ninety-by-ninety-inch titan of the tall timbers. Such individuals, when they want a lighter bag, may prefer the more conventional rectangular sacks; these run on up from thirty inches wide when closed, and in some excellent, all-waterfowl-down models, weigh less than four pounds. A large man, six feet or over, will find a bag forty inches wide or more a lot more comfortable. You may have to hunch up on the hands to turn in these, too, but a few nights of this makes the process as natural as stepping over a log.

Air Mattresses

Maximum comfort is attained when one has an air mattress under an adequate sleeping robe. One of these requires only several minutes to inflate. The natural tendency among individuals accustomed to sleeping on the rather solid conventional bed is to pump their air mattress too full. It will be just about right if you will inflate it until you can just barely touch the ground when pressing down on the center with your fist. Another way to accomplish the same result is to pump in more air than you'll need and then lie on it on your side and open the valve until your hipbone just touches the hard surface beneath. A small light rubber pump is convenient for inflating; the bulb attachment can be worked by either hand or foot.

If weight and space are important considerations, a good air mattress to secure is one about four feet long by half as wide. This should be located just beneath the shoulders and hips. Browse, leaves, brush, or anything else suitable, such as a horse blanket, may then be used to level off under the head and legs.

The stability afforded by this last evening-off of the

sleeping surface generally eliminates any tendency there may be to roll off the mattress during the night. Poles or even a couple of large rocks can always be placed at either side of the bed to keep everything in position. Once the average individual has slept out on such an arrangement for several nights, however, he won't have any trouble in making his bed stay put. Most never do experience any difficulty.

If a little additional bulk and weight will pose no problem, and if the amount of use you plan to get out of the bed softener will justify the added expense, by all means secure the best available full-length air mattress. These are particularly excellent for cabin use.

All air mattresses are by themselves cold in frosty weather, a shortcoming which can be entirely overcome by spreading some insulation, such as a fur robe or spare woolens, between the mattress and the robe. This disadvantage is more than offset by the unexcelled coolness the air mattress affords during the hot months.

An air mattress should be laid on a hard, flat, rigid surface. There is no need to bother removing minor irregularities; the mattress will automatically adjust to them. However, some of the more fragile models need something such as a tarp between them and rough ground for protection against puncture.

One occasionally sees these mattresses being used on a sagging bunk or cot, to the discomfort of the occupant. Sleeping on the floor above an air mattress is far more relaxing. A bunk or cot can be adapted for air mattress use, though, by providing it with a solid surface of boards or poles.

A lightweight foam mattress is as functional as an air mattress.

Pillow

You may find that some sort of a pillow will add greatly to your comfort. This may be a folded shirt. It may be a pillow case that you stuff with dry pine needles or wild marsh hay. It may be an air pillow that you can blow up by mouth in a few seconds. One of these weighs but an ounce or so and can be carried in a game pocket during wet weather to double as a dry seat.

10. Woodsman's Tools

The most indispensable tool for a hunter, fisherman, or camper, and in fact for any outdoor man, boy, woman, and girl anywhere, is the knife—a businesslike knife, sharp and keen. Mrs. Whelen's aunt, who taught high school Latin for thirty years in Nebraska, had the right idea. She asked every class, "Which of you boys has a jackknife in your pocket?" The ones who had none did not rate very high with her.

Her thinking was that if a boy did not have a knife and know how to use it, he was not likely to grow up able to do many things for himself. And an outdoorsman has to be capable of doing *everything* for himself, unless he everlastingly ties himself to the apron strings of a guide—and then he is not an outdoorsman.

Cooks' Knives

You need a knife constantly afield, and for many purposes. For example, the camp cook will require one for slicing bread and meat, paring vegetables, and for a dozen other chores. Any fair-sized knife will do for such duties. It is better to have a special one for kitchen work, however, as this blade is almost sure to get such rough treatment that it would take a lot of labor to keep it sharp enough for other jobs.

Furthermore, a cook's knife both performs and holds up better when not given the fine edge desirable for pocket and hunting knives. One reason for this is that breadstuffs are sliced and meat carved more easily with what is actually a sawing action. When viewed under a strong magnifying lens, the coarse edge made by sweeping the blade forward a few times against a carborundum diagonally from heel to tip, first on one side and then on the other, actually resembles the teeth of a saw. This edge can be quickly renewed by the same process.

An ordinary, small butcher knife goes well with most outfits. Have a sheath for it, and keep it in the bundle with the knives, forks, and spoons.

The best all-around type is the so-called trapper's knife, made by most large cutlery concerns, with one blade for rough usage and another for finer work in closer quarters. The first blade, with a rounded point, is excellent for general skinning. The second blade, with a point sharp enough to lift a splinter from your hand if need be, can be kept for the more delicate skinning around eyes and ears and also for small animals. Whatever other knife you have, you'd better have one of these that you can keep in your pocket always. We've both had knives like this in our back pants pockets ever since we were knee-high to a chopping block.

Sheath Knives

While the trapper's claspknife will do everything necessary for the outdoor sportsman, many of us, particularly if we hunt big game, find it handy to carry a sheath knife.

Almost all interest in outdoor knives revolves around this type. There are some who think it is a sort of Billy the Kid weapon, and that one on the belt marks its owner as a tenderfoot. But there is no law against carrying it in the rucksack, if you prefer, or tying it safely out of the way on a saddle. If, for some reason, you want to wear it in the wilderness where you can get at it most easily, there's no proviso against that, either, and under certain conditions this practice could come in plenty useful.

The trouble is that most sheath knives one sees are entirely too large, long, and thick-bladed to be practical. The sheath knife with which we are here concerned is primarily for the hunter's use. It should be designed chiefly for skinning and butchering animals. At the same time, it should also be good for all reasonable outdoor purposes. A sheath knife can be invaluable for a lot of different jobs: blazing, cutting browse, repairing leather goods, and making fuzzsticks for starting a fire.

If you spend much time in remote regions, you'll also want one that you can depend on in any number of possible emergencies, such as cutting a fallen horse loose from a tangled picket rope or driving the knife into solid ice for a handgrip after you've fallen through into a wilderness lake.

It is true enough that you can skin out the biggest moose and bear with nothing more than a tiny penknife. You can do it better with a sharp and thin small blade, as a matter of fact, than with a dull and thick large blade. But a fine sheath knife makes such jobs a lot easier. Many old-time hunters, for that reason, prefer to keep their sheath knives really sharp for hunting alone. They usually prefer a blade not more than from four to six inches long, with the edge straight until it curves to the point.

A rounded point, rather than a sharp spear end, makes

for easier skinning. A thin blade that tapers all the way from the back to the cutting edge will take a much keener edge, and you can work faster and easier with it than with a blade that is thick from back to middle and which then tapers sharply to a wedge.

My own knife that I have always carried when hunting since 1916 was made by hand from a Green River butcher knife, and it has served my every need well. The mountain men of a century ago used Green River knives, and I call mine "Seeds-ke-dee," which is the old Indian name for the Green River of Wyoming.

We both have custom knives, made to order by hand by W. D. Randall, Jr. I think they are the finest knives I have ever seen, although they are rather costly. The size and shape of handles and blades are just about right, to my way of thinking. Brad swears by them. If I were wearing a new knife, I would choose one of these. But I guess I will stick to Seeds-ke-dee to the end for sentiment's sake and because of all the good it has done me. I am eventually going to give it to Brad.

THE SHEATH

You will want a substantial leather sheath to protect both the knife and yourself. Safely strapped in such a container, the tool may then be carried on your belt, in rucksack, duffel bag, saddle pocket, or wherever you wish. In any event, it will be advisable to make sure that the sheath is well made and if necessary reinforced, perhaps with copper rivets that you can add easily enough youself.

Points have a way of cutting themselves loose, particularly after a sheath has been accidentally cut at the top, with the result that the blade sets in deeper than intended. When points are so exposed, they may drive into your leg or hip should you fall, and there is even more constant danger that they may slash a hand. Some of us find it advisable, in addition to adding rivets, to stitch the lower part of the sheath with copper wire, making sure that the ends of this are worked off in such a way that they will not scratch.

Oiling sheaths is commonplace. It is not a desirable practice, however, because of the way it softens the leather. Not only is the knife then difficult to sheathe, but the point has a tendency to catch and to puncture the flexible and often curling leather. Saddle soap is preferable for preventing the leather from becoming too dry. Ordinary shoe polish is good, too, and is also the application to use if you desire a darker and less conspicuous base.

Knife Steel

Anyone who has used and sharpened knives for some time will recognize good steel the moment he touches the blade to a whetstone. There is something indefinable in the way a good blade takes hold and slides on a whetstone, and this is soon detected after you have tried to sharpen a few good knives and some poor ones.

For a general-purpose knife, and particularly for a hunting knife, avoid those with stainless steel blades. They may be all right for fish and table knives, but ordinarily they won't take a keen edge. When they are dull it takes forever and a day to bring them to even half-decent sharpness on a whetstone.

Stainless steel knives made by hand are harder than mass manufactured products, for a tougher metal can be used than can be handled by die stamping. But usually, if you are going to put out the money for a hand-made knife, you may as well have the very finest high carbon steel.

It is true that all carbon steel blades are stained by the acids in meat. This discoloration does not injure the metal, however. It can be polished off with crocus cloth if that seems desirable.

Sharpening Stones

A knife, ax, and any other edged tool should be kept sharp for best and safest results. Knives, when they come from the makers, do not usually have a keen edge, and these should be honed before use. It does not suffice merely to sharpen your knife before you start on your trip. It will continue to dull whenever used, the dreams of advertising writers to the contrary, and it will require sharpening a proportionate number of times afield.

Skinning an animal takes the edge off a blade very quickly. When dressing out a grizzly, for example, you probably will need to sharpen the ordinary knife one or two times; not a Randall! In fact, one of the first things most of us do when coming up on a kill is to lay our carborundum in some handy spot so that we won't have to start digging gingerly for it in a few minutes with slippery fingers.

Axes

The ax is an almost indispensable tool for the woodsman, many of whom rate it even above matches as the most valuable item to have along in the bush. It may be, nevertheless, a very dangerous instrument in the hands of a novice.

The ax is not really needed in the average warm weather camp. It is not necessary, either, on summer backpacking trips where at most the lighter short-handled hand ax will serve every purpose. The ax is rather the tool for heavy work, for getting in large wood for fires, for building big shelters, and for cutting out timber that may fall across trails and canoe streams.

The ax with a two-and-one-half or perhaps a three-pound head is big enough for most sportsmen. Heavier axes bite deeper and therefore, in the hands of an expert, do faster work. This is why lumberjacks, frontiersmen, and others who grow up in ax country and use these mobile wedges regularly throughout the years pick heavy models. These, besides being tiring in the hands of a tyro, require a lot of skill and are therefore potentially more dangerous.

Double-bitted axes are very tricky tools in the hands of all but experienced and careful men. In addition, they cannot be used as hammers, for which purpose (although it is not to be recommended) the camper is sometimes apt to find himself employing it a dozen times a trip.

The handiest ax for packing is the Hudson Bay model with a narrow butt and a face of normal width. You see an occasional craftsman using one of these painstakingly on a log cabin, but such an individual is usually a perfectionist who has more of the qualities of the cabinet maker than of the carpenter. This model, because of its narrow poll through which the handle is attached, does not hold up too well in all cases.

But for ordinary camping requirements, where weight is a factor and you still want an ax, a Hudson Bay with a one-and-one-half-pound head and a twenty-four-inch handle will do a lot of work. A metal-riveted leather sheath should ordinarily be added. The Hudson Bay ax, incidentally, is a convenient one to tie behind your saddle.

If you are going to be using an ax very much, you will

probably be most satisfied with an ordinary single-bit ax with about a two-and-one-half-pound head. A handle or helve about twenty-six to twenty-eight inches long is generally enough, though some may find they can swing the thirty-six-inch handle more naturally. In any event, if you adopt one length of handle and use it exclusively, you will come to do better and safer work.

It was in 1901 that I first had to do a lot of chopping. My ax had a twenty-seven-inch handle, and ever since I have wielded this length. My collaborator's experience has been the same, and he's spent numerous winters in a log cabin in the north woods where temperatures occasionally plummet so low that a saw blade shatters instead of bending and an ax not warmed beforehand can sliver to fragments against an icy chunk of green wood.

I have not used many axes, only three I think, but these have gone through a pile of logs. If you use an ax decently, it almost never wears out, although you will have to replace the handle now and then.

The edge on the ax you buy is probably sharp enough for the average two-weeks-a-year camper. The good axman will probably want to thin this edge for keener cutting. The best tool for this, and for rough sharpening as well, is a grindstone, kept wet during use. In the woods a ten- or twelve-inch flat file does a good job. To sharpen an ax, start about an inch back from its edge and carry that out straight. Taper very slightly to the edge itself, but do not overdo this or the ax will bind. Finish the job with a carborundum stone.

AXMANSHIP

A whole volume could be written on the subject of axmanship. Our best axman almost all picked up the art as

AXMANSHIP

A. Chop at an acute angle to the grain.

B. The ax, hitting at a right angle in the grain, will hardly bite at all.

C. The way to chop limbs off a trunk.

D. Start each of the pair of notches needed to chop a fallen log in two as wide as the log itself. Two such Vs, joining at the stick's center, will sever it most economically.

E. To fell a tree in the direction of the arrow, begin notch 2 as a safety measure. On the opposite side, cut notch 1 about three-fifths through the trunk. Deepen notch 2 until the tree begins to fall, and then stand aside at an already chosen point of safety.

Keep your ax sharp. A dull ax makes slow and hard work and is liable to glance.

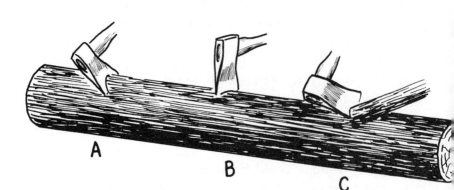

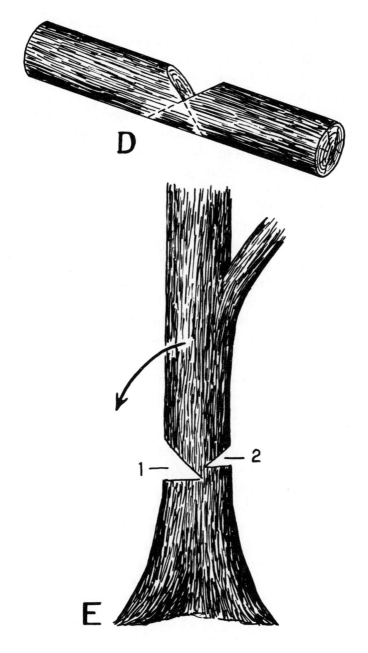

D

E

1 — 2 —

boys on the farm or in the woods, but with practice and care anyone can learn well enough for all the usual camp chores. Incidentally, if you've played much golf, you'll find the desirable free and easy swing to an exact point almost second nature.

The main thing is to be careful. You can ruin a hunting or fishing trip mighty easily with just one stroke that lands a fraction of an inch from where you want it to go. The best general precaution is to anticipate the worst and to be so placed that even if it does occur no one will be hurt. Too, a sharp ax is safer than a dull one in that it is not so prone to bound off the wood.

Be prepared to have the ax glance off a knot, and have your feet and legs where they will not be hit. Take the time to clear away any shrubs or branches that might catch the blade, instead of relying on a perfect swing. Don't take the risk of steadying a billet with a hand or foot.

Avoid, too, the common practice of leaning a stick against a log and half chopping and half breaking it in two. A lot of head injuries from flying wood have resulted from that all-too-prevalent habit. When you're felling a dead tree for firewood, watch out that another tree doesn't break off the top and send it crashing back toward you. In other words, there are a great many possible misadventures. The more of these you can foresee and protect yourself against, the less will be the possibility of an injury.

When you stop to think of it, axes are far less dangerous than such a very common substance as glass. Any shortcomings do not lie in the ax but, rather, in the individual. Use this wedge with a nice easy swing. When chopping with an ax, let gravity do most of the work, and you'll be able to cut all morning without pressing. Keep your eye on the exact spot where you want the edge to strike, and practice until it does always strike there.

FELLING TREES

Even the most inexperienced cheechako can drop his first tree almost exactly where he wants it to fall if he will follow the few very simple principles set forth here. He will, of course, have to take into consideration such external factors as wind, tilt, weight, and nearby objects. He will do well, too, to start on trees small enough that their fall can be guided to some extent, if need be, by hand.

First of all, cut a small safety notch as insurance against the tree's splitting or the butt's kicking backwards. Slightly below this safety notch, on the opposite side of the tree (the side where you want the timber to fall), chop a wide notch. When this cut is about three-fifths through the trunk, a few cuts at the first nick should be enough to send the tree toppling.

These two notches are so located, as can be seen by the illustration, that they provide a hinge. This hinge not only directs the way in which the weight of the tree will cause it to fall, but it also lessens the possibility that the butt may slide perilously backward on the stump. It is advisable, however, to have a safe place already picked out and to hasten there when the fibers start their final cracking.

It is even easier to drop a tree by using a saw. The principles remain the same. You make the same brief initial cut. You follow it with a deep slit opposite and below. You then deepen the first incision. An ax, or perhaps a wooden wedge cut on the spot, may have to be driven into one gash or the other to free the saw. Too, you can often topple a heavy tree that is pretty much on balance and come closer to pinpointing its fall by using a wedge in the higher cut.

Hatchets

The light one-pound ax with a twelve-inch handle will do about all the work necessary in the summer or auto camp and on backpacking trails. The average camper will use it with more effectiveness and greater safety than he will a long-handled ax. As a matter of fact, some of the more skillful backwoods ax men often turn to such a hatchet. Up in the Peace River country, Charlie Ohland, the best ax man we know of, can smooth off a pole or log so skillfully with a light hatchet that you'd suppose it planed.

Such a hand ax can come in useful when you're butchering, although you'll have to touch up the blade afterward. It works well enough in securing wood for a small campfire, and it's a lot more useful than a knife for blazing a trail. Secure a substantial sheath for it, but don't carry it on your belt. This is both inconvenient and uncomfortable. Stow it instead in a rucksack or saddle pocket.

Saws

It is usually much easier and faster to saw all but small logs than it is to chop them. If you are using a wood-burning stove, such a tool will be invaluable for working available fuel into the right lengths to fit the firebox. Even when you're bivouacking in weather nippy enough to argue the companionship of an overnight blaze, a saw will make the task of accumulating enough fodder for that campfire a comparatively easy one.

The long slender blade of the swede saw is a favorite of campers, bivouackers, and sourdoughs in the cold climates. It is so light that it can be handled easily in any position. The long narrow blade is so flexible that, except during extreme cold, it can be coiled to the circumference of a saucer, held together by a cord wound and tied among its teeth, and wrapped with a piece of canvas for carrying. The two-piece, light, tubular handle is easily slid apart and packed.

Whatever saw you take with you into the bush, don't make the mistake that some tenderfeet do and carry a blade with the ordinary crosscut or rip teeth of the carpenter's tools. See to it that your saw is designed for cutting rough timber.

Repair Kits

Some kind of repair kit should be included in every camp outfit except perhaps that of a backpacker who has to pare everything down to the last ounce. Don't attempt to carry a whole shop with you, but include only those small articles that you think may be needed and for which nothing else will serve.

Everyone occasionally changes his opinions about what such a kit should include. After years of adding and discarding, here is what the two of us find in our own repair outfits:

A small set of fine screwdrivers, all nested within the handle of the largest.

A small flat-nosed pliers—something of this sort is especially advisable wherever a dog accompanies you in porcupine country. This also has a wire cutter for accidentally embedded fishhooks.

A small flat file for sharpening the ax.

A tiny can of assorted small nails, tacks, copper rivets, and buttons.

Thin copper wire, shoe thread, rawhide lace, a bit of wax, and a coil of light snare wire.

Various needles.

A tube of all-purpose adhesive.

Some nylon fishline.

We both carry very small saws that will whip through metal as well as bone. Once in a hardware store I found a light, metal pistol grip handle that would hold a short hacksaw blade. I bought it and a dozen blades. It has gone along on every trip since and has come in mighty handy a hundred times.

11. Footwear for Wilderness Trails

Much advice has been offered about the selection of footwear for extensive use in rough and difficult country. A great deal of this counsel, unfortunately, has come from those whose backgrounds have been more theoretical than practical. Many important considerations have been both misinterpreted and incorrectly emphasized, if not omitted entirely.

Additionally confusing is the understandable fact that not all the popular shoes offered and advertised are by any means desirable under many outdoor conditions. Salesmen, not always experienced and conscientious, are likely to urge the makes and sizes that are in stock.

The matter is a very serious one. The sportsman taking to the woods for perhaps the first time, on a trip that requires long and difficult foot travel, is too often apt to discover when it's too late that he is irrevocably committed to footwear that will handicap or badly cripple him, thus ruining the grand outing he may have been planning for years.

Perhaps this writer had better qualify as to experience. To a certain extent, I might be called a professional walker. I served twenty-two of my forty years of military service in the infantry. There we certainly hiked ten times as much over rugged terrain as the average hunter and fisherman. There, too, I had to attend not only to my own footwear and foot care; I also had to supervise that of large numbers of men under my command.

In this latter duty, I didn't feel I was in a position to make any mistakes. Staring at me over the years was this statement included by Horace Kephart in what was long the best and the most widely read and accepted of outdoor manuals. What Kephart wrote was: "Lieutenant Whelen, so well known to us as a sportsman and military authority, says of it [the Munson Army last]: 'In the light of what the army now knows, sore feet are absolutely inexcusable. The presence of sore feet in an officer's command is a cause for investigation as to the efficiency of that officer.'"

During the years since my retirement from active service I have, you might say, been a professional outdoorsman with a very large mileage of rough hiking in all kinds of country and climates.

Shoes and Socks

The shoe size you wear in the city, and the one that the ordinary salesman there will measure you for, will perhaps do well enough for the three or four miles of walking which is all many an individual covers on an outing. But beware of this size of shoe for a daily tramp of eight to twenty miles over wild country, even through fairly open bird cover if it is a bit hilly.

One such excursion in city-size footwear will almost certainly lay you up with blisters and abrasions. After three or four miles of tramping over rugged terrain, your feet swell considerably because of the repeated and varying pressure of walking and because of the stimulation of exercise. The shoes you select must be large enough to remain comfortable when your feet are in this enlarged condition.

The simple but all-important formula for wilderness walking is: heavy socks and big shoes. Regardless of heat or cold, dryness or wet, only wool socks are suitable for long hikes. These may vary from thin to medium during the summer and from medium to heavy during the frosty months. Throughout the year, however, you want only genuine, top-quality, finely processed, and well-made woolens. Don't have anything to do with the shoddy if you can possibly avoid it. Poor woolens mat. They contain impurities that irritate the feet. They wear poorly. As for loosely and skimpily knit socks, these are an abomination from the first day you put them on.

In regard to socks, three precautions will usually suffice. Wear only well-fitting and fairly new socks with no rough seams or unduly harsh darned spots. If your feet are tender, dust both them and your socks the first week with foot powder.

Wash your feet at least every night, and change your socks daily. When the going is rough, as a matter of fact, it is refreshing to stop when possible during the day and bathe the feet. A lot of us carry an extra pair of socks to switch to at that time.

Good woolen socks are easily washed, without shrinking, with soap and barely warm water. They should be rinsed, gently squeezed reasonably free of moisture without wringing, and stretched back into shape to dry slowly, preferably in an open breeze but in any event well back from the campfire.

A few people's skin seems to be allergic to wool. Such

individuals can often wear thin socks of some other material under the wool with advantage. These may be made of cotton. Some individuals select nylon, which is certainly long-wearing but which, for a lot of us, is a lot too slippery unless either worn too tightly or gartered in some manner, neither of which is compatible with the outdoor routine.

Taking the thickness of your socks into consideration, here is a general rule you can apply in selecting the ideal size of footwear for hard outdoor wear. With one pair of thin or medium wool socks, have your shoes one full size longer and one full size wider than your proper fit in city shoes. For heavy socks, have them one-and-one-half sizes longer and wider. If half sizes are not available, increase to the next full size. For the additional socks that may be desirable in extremely cold weather, experiment to get the same comparative freedom of fit as above.

Breaking In Footwear

It is highly important that you break in new outdoor footwear to fit your feet well in advance of a trip. Some of us have feet that are differently shaped from normal, such deformities being more or less caused by improper if stylish fittings of city shoes. The lasts on which good outdoor shoes are made are designed for normal not expanded feet. When the shoes are new, even though correctly fitted, they may bring undue pressure on parts of your feet. The new footwear will gradually stretch at these points, however, if broken in slowly and easily.

There are two functional ways of breaking in new leather shoes. You can do it gradually by hiking two miles the first day, three miles the second, and so on up to five miles, by which time the process should be completed. The second method consists of standing in four inches of water for fifteen minutes and then hiking until the shoes dry on your feet.

High-top Boots

Did you ever notice the shoes of the professional walker, the Alpinist, or the marching apparel of our infantry? You will find no high tops here. You'll see, rather, a height of not more than seven inches as measured in the rear from the bottom of the heel to the top.

High tops almost always sag and wrinkle more or less at the ankles. This can bring pressure to bear on the Achilles tendon at the back of your ankle. It is true that this becomes negligible in the case of gradually softened and well broken-in leather tops, and that in any boot the sagging can be offset to a large extent by inserting some stiffener, such as folded heavy paper or a piece of birchbark. Unless there is a definite and valid reason for high tops, however, the fact remains that this pressure, if not relieved, will set up a painful inflammation of the sheath through which this greatest tendon of our body runs. The only cure for this is ten days off your feet.

My regiment was issued a then new type of shoe with nine-inch tops, back in 1911, when the Army was experimenting with shoes. These were almost exactly like the majority of sportsmen's boots now advertised and illustrated. Shortly thereafter, my regiment was ordered on a 300-mile practice march to test this footwear. Thirty percent of the command suffered from this inflammation, medically known as synovitis. That ended the experiment.

There is also the weight factor. A boot with a ten-inch top will weigh about eight ounces more than one which is six inches high. That is an additional half-pound to be lifted 3 inches high and to be carried 28 inches ahead about 2,500 times every mile. Such additional expenditure of energy tells like the dickens on a long, all-day tramp.

Get your hiking shoes six inches, or not over seven inches, high. Leave the high-top boots for horsemen, for exceptionally wet and muddy country, and for bad snake regions. Paratroopers wear high boots for other reasons, and they have little walking to do.

Bird-Shooter Shoes

These are oiled leather shoes, usually of imitation as well as true moccasin types with composition soles and heels. The true moccasin shoe, of course, is built about a single piece of leather which extends all the way under the foot. Beneath this entity, the sole is attached. To make sure that a shoe is a true moccasin, look and feel inside the toe to ascertain if a single area of leather forms both bottom and sides.

This footwear is made by a dozen manufacturers of sporting shoes under many different names. Worn with thin or medium woolen socks, such shoes are very satisfactory for bird shooting and in general for long hikes over trails. In fairly steep country, however, they should have soft crepe or heavily cleated rubber soles.

Being fairly light, they make quite satisfactory footwear for hunting mountain game in the higher western mountains when they are provided with suitable soles, which we will discuss in a moment.

Army Marching Shoes

The old-type marching shoes used by our infantry are of leather with the smooth side turned functionally in and the rough side forming the exterior. There is no lining. The soles are usually composition. The shoes are only six inches high and are made on the Munson Army last—in my estimation, the best that has ever been devised for the normal American man's foot.

These shoes can usually be obtained from any of the many dealers in Army surplus goods and at what are usually very reasonable prices. All the remarks about bird-shooter shoes apply to these, also.

Rubber Bottoms and Leather Tops

Shoes with rubber bottoms and leather tops are made by many manufacturers. For practically all wear, unless there is a definite reason to the contrary, they should be purchased with tops only six or seven inches high. For extremely wet country, like Newfoundland, where in many areas you sink in several inches of water with almost every step, the tops had better be eight inches, In muskeg areas of the continental Northwest, where even in winter the periodic chinooks and the almost constant overflow make for slushy going, you may have a real need the year around for tops as much as ten inches high.

These boots should be worn with insoles and one or more pairs of wool socks. It's not a bad idea to get an extra pair of insoles so that a dry pair will be available each day. Felt is a favorite. For those who do not care for the flat-footed sensation that is characteristic of most such rubber-bottomed shoes, leather insoles with arch-support steel shanks are available, if you want them. For very cold weather, these may be secured with clipped lambskin next to the feet. L. L. Bean, Inc., of Freeport, Maine, is one supplier.

The better boots of this sort are ideal for deer and other big-game hunting in the fall, except in the steepest country, because they are almost noiseless and because they can be kept water-repellent clear to the top. They can also be used in winter, although rubber gets pretty cold around twenty degrees below zero and a steel stirrup feels mighty frosty when the thermometer drops much below that range.

One of us, however, has consistently found rubber-bottoms preferable in low temperatures. Often in such cold, hidden overflow from brooks and rivers can be a serious problem, for regular channels freeze in the intense cold and water is forced to the surface, where many times it spreads concealed under thin ice and snow. With lambskin insoles and two pairs of heavy socks, such boots are not too cold.

Throughout eastern Canada, low-top rubbers are donned practically universally, and even the Indians are coming to prefer them to moccasins during summer and fall. More and more trappers and prospectors in the North are shifting to them. When the rubber bottoms wear out, you can have new shells attached to the leather tops at a considerable savings.

They're not good for wear in the very steep mountains of the West, particularly not on steep snow-covered slopes. I darn near broke my fool neck, and did sprain my ankle, on such a precipitous incline in Montana some years ago when wearing them. They are treacherous on smooth ice, too, although for traversing occasional short stretches encountered during a trip, creepers or light crampons can be used to offset this hazard. For deer and moose country and for northern canoe routes, they are the most satisfactory of all footwear.

Mountain Boots

Mountain boots are for use in the steep mountains of our continental West and Northwest; for the rougher country off the usual hiking trails; for climbers; and for the hunting of sheep, goat, and grizzly in the taller ranges. Boots for such terrain were not obtainable ready-made in the United States until recently. Mountain climbers usually imported their footwear from Europe and from two Canadian makers.

For climbing in the higher peaks where precipitous rock, snow, and ice conditions must be bested, the shoe should be of the heavy Alpine type. The Alpinist does not usually hike for miles. His daily efforts, rather, are short if severe. He needs a shoe that can be planted, pounded down hard, and that will stick right there.

The hunter of big game in tall mountains needs a slightly lighter shoe. His day's hunt may take him many miles. Almost certainly, however, he will come on dangerously perpendicular country, particularly in the final stalk for mountain game. There he must not slip. The soles of his mountain hunting shoes should be similar to those of the Alpinist, or he will run great risks of a crippling fall if not death.

To that both of us can strongly testify. I've already mentioned my experience in Montana. The first Stone Mountain sheep Brad shot, he stalked while wearing rubber bottom boots. The only way he could work his way across some icy slants that dropped off in nothing more substantial than ozone was by driving his Randall hunting knife into the crust and using it for a handgrip until he could set himself sufficiently to repeat the procedure.

If you will examine the hoofs of mountain sheep and goat, you will see that the outer rim of each hoof consists of a hard shell with a sharp edge where it makes contact with the ground. The interior of the hoof has a comparatively soft pad not greatly unlike crepe rubber. The entire foot is a fine example of how the sole of a safe mountain shoe should be constructed.

HOBNAILS OR RUBBER CLEATS

Two types of soles are preferred, each having its advocates. There are the hobnailed varieties. Hobnails can be applied to any of the bird-shooter or Army marching shoes, providing these have leather soles. Nails and calks will not, of course, stick in either composition or rubber bottoms. Hobnailed boots are excellent for Alpine climbing, particularly on ice and glaciers, although they are a little noisy for hunting.

My own experience in hunting and climbing throughout British Columbia and Alberta has indicated that the hobnails are best arranged as shown in the accompanying sketch. The square Swiss edging nails are placed an inch apart around the edge of the sole and heel. The sharp square edges of these heavy nails insure against front, back, and side slipping on any surface except hard, smooth rock.

These Swiss edging nails you may obtain from our leading sporting goods outfitters who cater to mountain climbers. Your bootmaker or cobbler will be able to install them. They should be cleated all the way through the edge

Pattern for hobnailing boots: the square Swiss edging nails are placed an inch apart around the edge of the sole and heel; the ordinary one-headed nails are placed in the center of the sole and heel.

of the sole outside the uppers. The round interior nails shown are ordinary cone-headed hobnails which are procurable anywhere. They prevent slipping to some extent. Their principal function, however, is to keep the inside of the sole from wearing too fast. They should be cleated through the outer leather sole only, never through the inner sole, or they will eventually dig into your feet uncomfortably.

This means an extra job for the shoemaker. Regardless of this, make certain that he does not cleat these through the inner sole. Hobnailed soles are very safe, satisfactory, and durable. The only problems they present are that they are sometimes noisy for hunting and that you should remove them before entering a house, for they literally "play hob" with floors.

Many experienced mountain men are coming to prefer heavily cleated or lugged rubber soles which can be applied to any suitable leather sole by practically any shoemaker. These have cleats or lugs about one-half to one inch square that project at least half an inch below the rubber sole proper and stick well on all steep pitches and in snow. They are superior to hobnails on smooth rock although not on ice. Furthermore, they can be almost noiseless.

MOOSE MOCCASINS

Genuine Indian moosehide moccasins are not made commercially nor, for that matter, in quantity anywhere. It has been our experience that the only places a pair or two of these usually can be obtained are little trading posts and occasional trailside stores away back in the sticks in western Canada and Alaska. Nearby squaws make a few for sale at the post, and a few white women with time on their hands also turn out an occasional set. We both have often secured moosehide moccasins of our own from such sources, occasionally leaving an outline of a stockinged foot before heading into the bush, and picking up the finished products upon our return. Fit is not all that critical, however, and we've also done well enough from stock numerous other times. If you go north, you will also probably find yourself able to secure a pair by one of these two methods.

Imitation moosehide moccasins are merely tourist junk. On the other hand, moccasins made of oil-tanned leather by our better bootmakers are for most purposes far more practical than the moosehide varieties. They wear longer. There is no comparison in the way they retain their shape. They are not ruined by repeated wettings. They are less expensive.

In fact, you see a lot of the manufactured types these days at even the more remote trading posts. More and more, the Indians don't want to be bothered with the work. The high price of red squirrel fur in much of the moccasin country is one reason. It's considerably easier to snare or shoot, then process, two or three red squirrels, than to make a pair of moccasins worth the same amount.

In the sub-Arctic, however, many Indians are still partial to their own moccasins when they can get the skins, because the footwear is then practically at hand except for necessary tanning and sewing. When the weather is at all moist, the Indians invariably wear a husky pair of the white man's rubbers over the moccasins. These rubbers are identical with the heavier rubbers seen on city pavements during rainy weather.

Moosehide moccasins wet through as soon as you start to walk over even slightly damp ground. They become, at the same time, almost unbelievably slippery. It is, for example, a considerable task to get up a dew-glistening slope while wearing moccasins.

The moccasin plus the rubber is similar, in principle, to our leather-topped lumbermen's rubber. As a matter of fact, numerous aborigines these days wear the latter article much of the time.

But in the dry snow and the subzero cold of the Far North, it is another matter entirely. There the basic footwear of hunters and trappers, both white and native, is the locally made moccasin. This is usually large enough to be worn with several pairs of thick woolen socks.

The way one of us customarily travels when temperatures drop thirty degrees or more below freezing is with two heavy pairs of woolen stockings sandwiching moosehide moccasins, and finally low heavy rubbers. The feet not only keep warm this way, but they remain dry. When it is time to go into a cabin, the customary procedure is to remove the outer socks and the rubbers, shaking and beating them free of snow and leaving them outside. Sometimes, depending on snow conditions, a second pair of moccasins is worn directly beneath the rubbers, and then these are treated as outdoor wear.

A variation of this practice, witnessed among both whites and natives, is the use of ordinary fabric overshoes for the outer clothing. A third pair of socks is then ordinarily worn directly beneath the overshoes and is removed and left outdoors before one enters a warm cabin. If the individual is going to remain inside for a considerable length of time, of course, the outer wear is brought inside and warmed.

HOMEMADE MOCCASIN SOLES

When I was a youngster and hunted for that year and a half in the dry belt of British Columbia, living and traveling with several old mountain men and in touch now and then with bunches of Indians, we all wore buckskin moccasins. These always had a buckskin sole which we sewed to their bottoms with sinew or buckskin thongs. Whenever the sole wore through, we put on a new one. The sole lasted from three days to a week, depending on the weather and on how much traveling we did. One pair of moccasins would thus last over a month.

One of the old mountain men had a klooch, a squaw, and I used to trade her two deerskins for one tanned skin and then do my own resoling. (This ratio of exchange is still common in the backwoods today, incidentally.) We wore the moccasins with two pairs of socks. Your feet had to tough and then some, but moccasins were the most nearly perfect footwear imaginable for high dry country.

When the snows came, however, one could break one's neck wearing them in such terrain, although rough soles with cleats helped a little. But only a very sure-footed individual can cover steep snow country in moccasins with any safety.

The old plains Indians all wore soles on moccasins. See the exhibits in any large museum. Even so, the squaws were tanning skins and making moccasins all the time.

Native moccasins, in any event, are most delightful to change to when you come back to camp after a day afield. Even in the biggest city, their unforgettable woodsy odor imparted by hours of tanning over smoky fires takes one back to the sensations of the wilderness at dusk.

12. Fending Off the Insect Hordes

Former Supreme Court Justice William O. Douglas once remarked that horsemanship consists of the ability to remain unconcerned, comfortable, and on a horse—all at once. We likewise assert that a part of woodcraft consists of knowing how to remain unconcerned, comfortable, and at the same time in an area plagued with awful bugs.

Mosquitoes

Mosquito protection these days is easier than it ever has been before. This is fortunate, for the confounded buzzers are still the most common pests with which outdoorsmen are cursed.

In North America, mosquitoes are more or less prevalent from late May and early June until September in all country close to nonflowing waters, in which they breed. They may be only slightly annoying along the trout streams in New England or in the high open country where animals seek relief, but we've seen unbelievable millions actually blackening the sky in other regions. Our northlands and low coastal belts are usually the worst infested areas.

Ernest Thompson Seton, the naturalist, kept a record of their numbers on a journey he made to the Barren Lands of Canada. On a day in early July, he counted 400 mosquitoes on the back of a companion's coat. He then began to establish a standard by which to gauge their numbers as he proceeded north. He would hold up his bare hand for five seconds and count the number of mosquitoes on its back. At first there were five to ten. Every day added to their number. In mid-July, on Great Slave Lake, where the waters of the Peace River pause before continuing down the Mackenzie to the Arctic Ocean, there were fifty or sixty. Several weeks later, on the wet and treeless tundra, the figure rose from 100 to 125. There the insects settled on his tent in such numbers when the wind was not blowing hard that he estimated 24,000 were darkening the outside of the canvas while as many more hovered exasperatingly about the door.

Yet local conditions, such as dryness, cold, and occasionally a forest fire, sometimes operate to reduce or eliminate the mosquitoes in a particular locality. I spent one June and July in the well-watered Cascade Range in British Columbia, at elevations over 4,000 feet, and never saw a skeeter. The Athabasca River has always been noted as being one of the very worst mosquito rivers of the North, but a friend of mine canoeing from Jasper Park to Waterways in July of 1949 reported no mosquitoes.

Malaria, yellow fever, and occasionally other diseases are transmitted to human beings by mosquitoes. Anyone going into the southernmost portions of the United States, Mexico, or the tropics should know which mosquitoes carry these diseases, how they transmit them, and the precautions to be taken.

WHAT TO EXPECT FROM MODERN REPELLENTS

On any trip into skeeter country, take along plenty of mosquito repellent. The old pine tar products, many of which also contained citronella and maybe a little creosote to lend them at least an aspect of authority, used to get all over everything—and were not particularly efficacious, to boot. Many individuals, furthermore, used to object to their odors more than insects did.

The better of the modern products are colorless, nonirritating, and nearly odorless. Under ordinary conditions they really work, too, discouraging insects from alighting and deterring most of them from biting for from one to five or six hours, usually in ratio to how much you perspire.

Under mild conditions, they're even effective some inches away from the skin, keeping the majority of mosquitoes from hovering annoyingly near your ears. When skeeters are thick, though, you're going to have to rub the dope on exposed parts every half-hour or so, always keeping it away from where it will run into the eyes and mouth. You're also going to want to douse some repellent on your clothing as well, especially around the neck and ankles. The most effective of all insect repellents for mosquitoes, biting flies, ticks, chiggers, and fleas—as we've found in really rugged testing grounds in the Yukon, British Columbia, and Alaska—is N,N-diethyl-Toluamide. It is now marketed under various brand names. Rubbed on exposed flesh or sprayed on clothing, it is effective for several hours and is easily renewed.

Any repellent should be used according to the particular instructions accompanying it, especially as some can damage plastics and synthetic fabrics.

SMUDGES

Smudges of damp and green wood and vegetation will discourage mosquitoes and flies around camp, making it possible to cook and eat meals without having bugs in everything. If you travel with horses, they will find much comfort when standing in such smoke, which they soon learn to seek. A smudge may be very irritating to eyes and nose, but often it is far preferable to continual skeeter and fly attacks.

MUD PLASTERS

If an individual happens to get stranded without matches or dope in bad country, plastering his exposed skin with mud can save his life.

PICKING INSECT-FREE CAMPSITES

In mosquito country, do not camp on the edge of a brook, along a lake shore, or in thick woods. Get higher up, as far from nonrunning water as is convenient, and in the open where wind will carry mosquitoes and flies away. Often you will be immune on small islands or on points of land extending well into open water. A high-cut bank above a mountain river is usually good. So is an open ridge or high meadow near a small clear spring.

MOSQUITO BAR

With lean-to and other open shelters, a mosquito bar may be erected over the sleeping bag and its bottom edges tucked under the mattress. One way to put it up is atop stakes driven in at the four corners of the bed. Another method is to suspend it from the roof.

Thin flexible poles, too, may be bent and thrust into the ground on either side of the sleeping bag in such a way that they will curve over the upper half of it in an arc reminiscent of the roofs of the old covered wagons. This framework may be covered with a large piece of cheesecloth, large enough to drape on the ground for a least a foot all around, protecting the exposed upper part of the body.

BITEPROOF CLOTHING

Clothing in mosquito country should be such that mosquitoes will not be able to bite through it. You may even need garments that can be tied or otherwise fastened tightly around neck, wrists, and ankles. You'll be wise to avoid, at the same time, fabrics that don't breathe. Some of the new synthetics are particular offenders in this respect, making you feel after a mile or so as if you'd been immersed in a steam bath. A loose shirt made from one's own deerskins is, we've found, especially pleasant to put on along toward evening. It is not too warm if you wear nothing beneath it.

Mosquito head nets may be purchased which droop from the broad brim of the hat down over the face and head; the net either tucks in at the neck or, preferably, extends over the shoulders to tie under the arms. Easiest to see through is black. Amber is practical, too. Incidentally, blue is the color most attractive to skeeters.

Gauntlet gloves, either leather or canvas, may be necessary. Both these and nets are abominably warm in summer, but where mosquitoes are notably savage and aggressive, as in parts of the Arctic, they can be far preferable to the incursions of the winged pests. Even in the worst country, however, it is very often possible to stay comfortable by keeping to open ridges and along broad streams where there is usually a breeze.

Cleanliness

Any camper can do worse than copy the woodchuck, which is one of our cleanest animals, although most unjustly called a groundhog. His burrow never smells of anything but clover, grass, and clean earth. In it he has a blind alley, at the end of which he deposits all refuse and covers it with earth.

Remember that you are camping in God's clean country. Leave it as pure and unspoiled as you found it, and do not make it look like Hell. Take good care of yourself, and take good care of the places where you pitch your shelter. You'll return home healthier, and you and those who follow you will always have fine places in which to kindle your campfires.

13. Taking Care of Yourself

The chance of an accident or serious physical trouble in the wilderness, remote from medical care, is exceedingly small. It is much less than in a city, certainly, where accidents and infections are so often due to the carelessness or ignorance of others and not to any lapse on your own part. In God's unspoiled country, there is comparatively little probability of infection. If you take sensible precautions, mishaps and misadventures on trips back of beyond are like most other worries; they almost never happen.

Anyone with a serious organic weakness would be foolish to absent himself from ready medical aid. Someone with a weak heart, for example, should not plan a strenuous mountain or backpacking trip. This leaves accidents to consider, and most of these in the wilderness are the result of either falls or the ax, in that order. You cannot afford to take chances. Literally, watch your step.

First Aid Kits

The soldier constantly wears a first aid kit attached to his belt. This is for bullet wounds only. We think that it is entirely unnecessary and inadvisable for you to burden yourself with any such kit merely for a one-day trip away from your camp. You must, however, have a medical kit at your camp, along the lines of the sportsman's medicine kit described later in this chapter.

Snake-bite Kit

In a country where there are poisonous snakes, you should always have an adequate snake-bite kit in your pocket, because in the unlikely eventuality that you are bitten, immediate first aid will be essential. There is a Cutter Compak Suction Snake Bite Kit which takes up little more room than a 12-gauge shot shell and which answers excellently the demands of emergency treatment. Simply pocket the kit, which contains complete instructions, and don't worry. The mortality rate of bites treated with such a kit is less than 1 percent.

SPORTSMAN'S MEDICINE KIT

Whenever you go into the bush, it is wise to take along a small but reasonably comprehensive kit, to deal chiefly with such common accidents as might occur and with the minor ills liable to upset us mortals. Generally, this outfit should take care of most emergencies until the patient can be taken to a doctor. Based on our experience, or rather on the things we have known to happen to other campers, we suggest the following articles:

1 triangular bandage for exterior bandaging and slings

1 gauze bandage, 2 inches wide in sterile package

6 gauze compresses, 3 inches square, each in sterile package

1 package assorted bandages

1 roll adhesive tape, 2 inches wide

1 tube sterile vaseline ointment for burns (Butter, lard, or saliva can cause very severe infections.)

1 bottle aspirin compound

1 bottle water purification tablets

1 cathartic, the kind you prefer

1 snake-bite kit

1 scissors, small and strong

1 tweezers, for splinters

2 razor blades

1 eyedropper

some large safety pins.

Being Your Own Wilderness Doctor by E. Russel Kodet, M.D., and Bradford Angier

Add anything else that your experience or that of members of your party indicate might be wise to take. Consult the authoritative book listed above and your own physician. The book directs you from symptoms to diagnosis, diagrams emergency surgical and bone-setting methods, suggests medicines, and protection against Tetanus, and prevents you from making dangerous treatment mistakes.

Freezing and Frostbite

A great many false notions surround the subject of cold weather. These range on up in potential seriousness from the often repeated assertion that during extremely frigid spells, saliva will freeze between the lip and the ground. In fact, saliva gives no sign of freezing in mid-air at better than 100 degrees below.

Another common but more dangerous error in reasoning is the basis of the widely proffered warning that when caught outdoors in very cold weather, you shouldn't let yourself fall asleep or you'll never awaken, freezing to death. The exact opposite is true. To put it briefly, passing over the obvious effects to be expected from excessive perspiring and from exhaustion, the only way the human system can manufacture the warmth needed to offset cold is by burning calories. The reserve of these energy units available for this need will be greatly lessened if, as many advise, we're consuming the calories by aimlessly walking around a tree all night.

The ideal, of course, is to get a good fire going and then lie up in its reflected warmth. The next best procedure is to hole up while you're dry and fresh in as sheltered a spot as you can find, curl or hunch as comfortably as possible on something dry such as bark or boughs, and relax as much as possible. If you fall asleep, the increasing coldness will finally awaken you just as it does in your own bed. You stir around just enough to get warm, which is often all you do at home, and then you relax again and maybe grab another nap. From a perspiration-chilled sleep of exhaustion that is too often the result of trying to keep going, there is many times no awakening.

The same sort of good judgment can be applied to the

widely reiterated nonsense that the way to thaw a frozen cheek is to rub it with snow. First of all, thawing frozen flesh by friction is at best an extremely slow process and one that is apt to compound the damage by tearing the sensitized area. Second, rubbing the skin with snow under such conditions is like scrubbing your face with gravel. Third, how can applying frozen snow to the frozen cheek be expected to accomplish anything except perhaps to extend the freezing?

Warmth is, of course, what is needed. To thaw a frozen cheek on the trail, hold a warm hand over it. To thaw a frostbitten finger, shove it under a warm armpit. To thaw a foot that has started to freeze, build a fire if you can do so quickly. Otherwise, keeping as well covered as you can, hold it against a warm part of the body, such as directly against the bare thigh. If a companion is with you, the thing to do is to thrust the foot against his bare abdomen. A horse, dog, or freshly killed trophy may also afford a solution.

Don't ever make the terrible error of trying to thaw a part of the body by immersing it, as has been done, in some liquid such as oil or gasoline which has been stored at subzero outdoor temperatures. Although far colder than 32° Fahrenheit, these and other fluids have sometimes been so used in the disastrous belief that because they themselves were not frozen, they were just the things with which to painlessly thaw something else.

Freezing, like every potential danger in the wilderness, isn't actually much of a threat to an experienced outdoorsman except as it may result from accidents. Against these, you habitually take simple but ample precautions. Your own inbred ingenuity and resourcefulness, stimulated by the instinct for survival, takes care of the rest. Besides, it has been said that a man sits as many risks as he runs.

14. Always Knowing Where You Are

It is all very nice, if you have the wherewithal, to employ a professional guide on your hunting and fishing trip into the back country. He will make camp for you, and do the cooking and many other chores, permitting you to devote the maximum time to hunting, fishing, photography, or just plain loafing. He will even guide you to the best hunting and fishing grounds, point out the game or bait your hook, and smilingly have the lunch out of his packsack at midday. When it's time to return to camp, he'll show you the way.

The owner of a big sporting camp once told us that none of his patrons ever went home without a deer. "How many sportsmen shoot their own deer?" we asked him. "You ought to know," he replied. "About one-third are babes-in-the-woods, and the guides shoot a deer for them."

But I guess we're both rather old-fashioned. We have always thought that the charm of life in the open lies in the complete liberty of action that it affords. The intrinsic allure of outdoor living, it has always seemed to us, is caught up in the satisfaction of being your own master and in the deep-down pride that comes from being able to look out for yourself under any circumstances and in any country or climate.

No one is going to feel confident, relaxed, and utterly at home in the bush until he understands the few very simple principles of finding his way anywhere and, alone or not, of always knowing for sure where he is.

There is nothing at all difficult about finding your way through strange wilderness, of always knowing the direction back to camp, and of never getting lost. It is downright easy, in fact, for staying found is just a matter of plain common sense and of keeping your wits about you.

But, first, let's disabuse ourselves of the commonest of the several utterly false notions that have been formed about this all-important part of woodcraft. No man is born with the innate ability to find his way out and back through country entirely strange to him. This prowess may be acquired. It is not instinctive. Neither does any human being carry a compass in his head. Even the most intuitive native, who has spent all his years in wild places, can find his way without outside help only through regions with which he is thoroughly familiar.

The educated man, although he may have been born in the city and lived there most of his life, makes a far better explorer than any native, as has been proved innumerable times. One reason for this is the fact that knowing where you're going, being sure of where you are, and having the certain knowledge of how to get back are not matters of instinct and mumbo jumbo. They are, rather, an ever intriguing problem of distances and angles.

The formula for all this is not hard to understand. It is not difficult to learn. Everything you need to know is contained in these next few pages. As a matter of fact, most of it is in the next paragraph.

We stay found by always knowing just about where we are. This is not as complicated, or as contradictory, as it may seem at first glance. Even the most inexperienced greenhorn can keep track of his position by the use of a map, a compass, and a pencil. Every ten minutes, or every time he changes direction, will not at first be to often to bring that map up to date. What if you have no map? Then, using the camp or road from which you leave as the starting point, you draw one as you go.

The wisest old woodsman uses exactly the same technique, whether he is aware of it or not. His map is in his head, that's all. Sun, moon, stars, vegetation, and any number of other natural factors may be his compass—under, it should be thoroughly realized, favorable conditions.

The sun and the moon have always risen in the east and set in the west. Everyone knows that at midday in the United States and Canada the sun is in the south, and that at midnight so is the full moon. The new moon (concavity to the left) is in the west in early morning. The old moon is in the east. The two outer stars that form the bowl of the Big Dipper point to the North Star, which has the appearance of being about seven times as far from them as they are from each other.

When and How to Use a Compass

The only difficulty with these primitive ways of reckoning comes in cloudy, stormy, foggy, and otherwise obscure weather. Then everyone in strange country needs a magnetic compass. Moss does not grow on the north side of trees often enough to be a reliable indicator, and a prevailing wind is apt to change direction without being noticed. Even in familiar wilderness, a compass will often save a lot of time that would otherwise be expended on trial and error.

There are many questions asked about a compass. Some people think a compass will point the way back to camp. It will do no such thing. All a compass can tell you is where is north—and where, reading clockwise, east, south, and west are located. But if you use your head along with your compass, you can keep from ever being turned around or bewildered.

Set any man at all down in country that is strange to him, without a magnetic compass on a day when he can't see sky or previously identified landmarks, and he will quickly get hopelessly turned around. What he'll then probably do, if he's an experienced outdoorsman, is camp until the weather clears. If any man tells you he never uses a compass, put it down that he never gets beyond country that is thoroughly familiar to him.

However, many woodsmen are so used to navigating in the way we're going to describe, they think they have an infallible sense of direction. If this were true, you could put them out from the south shore of Great Bear Lake in a canoe on a misty black night and they'd instinctively know exactly in which direction to paddle.

DECLINATION: HOW TO FIND IT AND ALLOW FOR IT

Using a compass is a very simple matter if you approach it with an open mind. If, in the United States and Canada, you place a magnetic compass away from metal on a flat surface and let the needle settle down, it will point north. That is, it will point to magnetic north. This is a shifting point up above Hudson Bay in extreme northeastern Canada, almost due north of the center of Ohio. In the state of Washington the needle points east of true north about twenty degrees. In Maine, the declination runs about twenty degrees west.

Although this is not technically exact, it is accurate enough in general for everday travel. Actually, the entire earth is a magnet, causing the declination to vary at different spots. In some localities, this may be as much as twenty-five degrees away from the magnetic shift indicated on ordinary maps.

To determine the declination from true north with fair accuracy, find the North Star. This lies almost exactly over the North Pole, being only slightly more than one degree away from precise north. You can then either note immediately the variation between almost exact north and where your compass needle is pointing. Or you can scratch a line pointing to the Pole Star, or indicate it by two stakes, and in daylight compare your compass to the thus established north-south mark.

The declination must be taken into consideration when you're reading a map. As a matter of fact, it is marked on many maps. If no compass directions are shown on the particular chart you are using, north may be assumed to be at the top, this being the way most are laid out.

What Compass to Buy

Your compass need not be an expensive model. Choose one, however, in which the north end of the needle is unmistakably marked, perhaps by being shaped like an arrow. Or you may prefer a compass whose entire dial moves.

Compasses are inexpensive. You may as well get a good one, although there is no need, nor is it advisable, to burden yourself with one of the elaborate surplus devices designed more for military use or for surveying. Get a good small compass, one that is rugged and preferably waterproof.

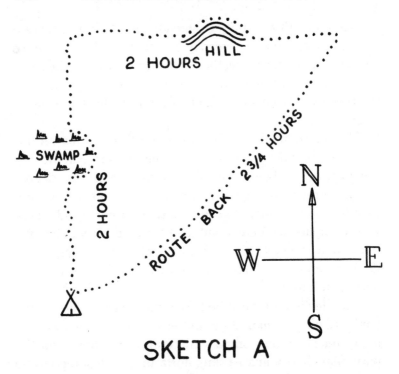

SKETCH A

In the wilderness, time is a more reliable indicator of distance than trying to estimate distance in miles.

Keep it where you will be sure not to lose it. In real wilderness, it's not a bad idea to carry a tiny spare. There is no good reason to buy a compass that does not have a luminous indicator.

Keeping a Map in Your Head

There are two kinds of maps. One is the map which you keep in your head as you go along. The other is the more or less accurate published map.

Your mind map, plus plain ordinary common sense, will keep you from getting turned around or lost. If for any reason whatsoever you have the slightest doubt of being able to retain this map accurately in your head, then sketch it on a piece of paper as you go along. Let us illustrate exactly how you do it.

Suppose you have camped the night before in a country utterly strange to you. It is now morning, and you elect to go hunting or trapping alone. You grab a lunch and, as shown in Sketch A, head north for two hours. In the wilderness as you will no doubt agree, time is a far more reliable indicator of distance than trying to estimate it in miles. Then for some reason best known to yourself, you turn to the right and hike east for another two hours. On the first course, you detour around a swamp. On the second, you curve around the base of a steep and rocky hill. You make allowances for both these detours in your time-distance record. At this point, it will be perfectly plain that if you travel a little less than three hours southwest over the same type of country, you will arrive right back at the camp from where you started.

The entire secret of finding your way and not getting lost lies in this little example. You must always know where you have gone and, by this knowledge, always approximately where you are. If you cannot rely on your memory, then it is only reasonable to sketch a map showing these two essentials.

Whenever you know where you have been and where you now are, you will always know the way back. This is not nearly as complex as it may sound. In fact, it is not complicated at all. You merely keep oriented and, using a watch if you want, you keep count of how far you go in each direction. The map, if you elect to draw one, can be as simple as Sketch A.

As you gain experience, following this procedure becomes more and more easy. But it is really foolproof from the start. That old woodsman, whose ability to find his way anywhere under all conditions you so admire, has used this system for so many years that it has become second nature to him. In all likelihood, he now follows it with scarcely a conscious thought.

Most of us have come across old bushmen who tell us that they find their way naturally and that they never get confused. Many of them insist on this until we pin them down with direct and pertinent questions. Then we always find that stored in their noodles are detailed and accurate mind maps.

Now, there are certain complications to this technique, as there are to every simple example. But as we come to each of these, you will see that the solution is in every instance merely a matter of sound judgment.

HOW TO USE RIVERS AND ROADS AS LANDMARKS

Suppose your camp is located beside a river, tote road, or some similar boundary. For purposes of illustration, let us assume that this landmark runs east and west, as indicated in Sketch B. A novice might think that he could hunt all day north of his boundry line, and then in late afternoon merely head south with the assurance that he would surely come back to it and then be able to follow the line to camp. But which way should he turn upon reaching the boundary? If he headed in the wrong direction, he might hike for miles and get nowhere.

The best technique in strange country is never to attempt to hit a blind objective, such as camp, on the nose. If you miss it, you'll have no better than a fifty-fifty chance of

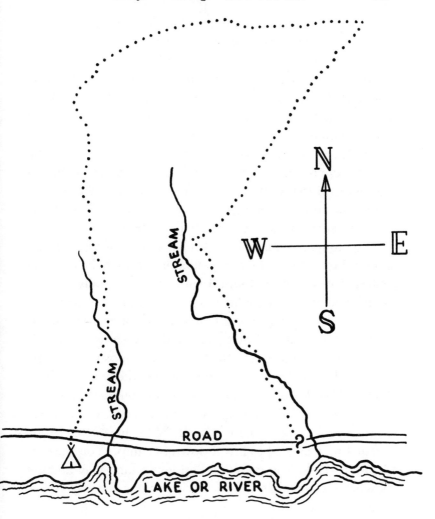

SKETCH B

If you are relying on the location of a long river to find your way back to camp, head out from camp positively in one direction of the river or the other. When you approach the river on the way back, you will be sure of which way to turn towards camp.

turning in the correct direction. For all practical purposes, the gamble is not even half and half. The human tendency, if you're not sure you've chosen the right way, is to give up too soon and turn back, only to have to come back over the same ground later. If, on the other hand, you bear positively to one side or the other of a long boundary, upon reaching it you will know for certain which way to turn.

There is one basic precaution to follow in this regard. Be sure of your road, river, lake, or other such boundary. Rivers cut back on themselves. Roads, particularly in the woods, sometimes come to abrupt ends in the midst of nowhere. Lake country can be particularly deceptive.

You may, of course, have a reliable map of the country, preferably checked by a dependable local inhabitant, that will resolve any such doubt. In any event, use only facts of which you are sure on which to base your procedure. If you have reached camp along that strange road, aim for the particular side of it of that you personally know.

When you start out in the morning, suppose you follow the little brook shown in Sketch B up into the hills. You hunt there all day, keeping a careful record of your directions and distances. Toward evening, on your way back, you come to a little brook. You think to yourself, "Why, here's that brook again. I may as well follow it down to camp." You start off along its bank. You go along beside it a long way and get nowhere. You realize that somewhere along the way you've miscalculated.

The trouble is that when you went up that brook in the morning, you did not note its various twists, formations, shores, bars, pools, chutes, and other peculiarities. If you had, when you came to that second brook in the afternoon, you would have soon realized it was not the same one. You would have oriented yourself and made a beeline for where you knew camp to be. You can still do that by, at worst, retracing your steps to where you went wrong.

This same general error can be made in relation to tote roads, game trails, watersheds, and other such features. It is best never to rely too positively on such landmarks but, instead, to stay oriented all the time and to keep track of your distances. Then you will always know just about where you are.

PROCEDURE IN DENSE FLAT COUNTRY

Suppose your camp is in dense level country where there are no landmarks. Suppose, for example, you are in thick jungle as were many of my camps when I was exploring in Central America. How are you going to leave camp in the morning, travel all day in trackless wilderness so thick that often you cannot see the flaming sun, and return to your outfit at night?

How to Make and Follow Blazes

The most practical procedure is to prepare for your return while still in contact with camp. You and your companions can do this by running blazed lines for a half-mile or so north, east, south, and west from camp. This will give you an objective, for all practical purposes a mile or so in diameter, at which to aim.

In this situation, be sure to keep very close track of your whereabouts. You will increase your margin for error by trying to hit this particular target plumb center. Once you have struck one of the four radii, you will be able to follow it right into camp. The higher blaze on the side of each tree towards camp ("h" igh for "h"ome) will show you which way to turn.

The usual blaze in the woods is made by chipping a piece of bark from a tree trunk so as to expose a conspicuous white patch of wood beneath. These are commonly at about eye level. (You sometimes come across a very high line of blazes in the north woods, puzzling until you realize they were made by a trapper on snowshoes.) Each succeeding spot, in any event, should be clearly visible from the one preceding. Changes of direction in particular should be clearly indicated.

For a temporary mark, you can break occasional small branches, taking care to leave the back route plainly evident. There is an understandable objection in national parks and forests to all varieties of marking which damage natural growth. The Appalachian Trail, for example, uses a dab of paint on trees and rocks to indicate trails.

PROCEDURE IN OPEN COUNTRY

The variations already considered, although they hold true everywhere, pertain mostly to wooded terrain where you cannot get much of an extended view and where each swamp, glade, and green-bedecked hill looks pretty much like every other. In the more open milieu that characterizes much of the continental West, it is generally far easier to keep track of your whereabouts. This is offset to a considerable degree, however, by the fact that uninhabited distances are often so tremendous and the country many times so stark and rough that one cannot afford to take chances. In some of the rugged mountains where we've camped, our objective has been in sight and yet more than a week away if we'd tried to walk straight to it. Under such circumstances, the important question often becomes less one of where camp is than of how to get there.

Let's assume that two miles due west of your camp there is a hill with a peculiarly shaped rocky prominence atop it. You can see this conspicuous eminence for miles. It will change its outline slightly as you travel. By keeping track of this, you can gauge just exactly where your camp lies in relationship to it. If you keep looking back and noting the appearance of things, you'll easily be able to journey back over the same route.

What to Do If Lost

If during your ordinary wanderings you suddenly discover you are not sure of your whereabouts, keep your shirt on and don't get excited. You are in no danger at all. You needn't even undergo any particular discomfort, especially if you have a knife and some matches that are safe from dampness. At the very worst, all you are in for is perhaps missing a couple of meals, and that is nothing.

The very real perils that can beset someone who is, or who believes himself, lost commonly arise from mental attitudes rather than from any physical circumstances. It is a disturbing comment on civilization that apparently stable city men, particulary first-time outdoorsmen, will sometimes lose all rationality when they are not sure of exactly where they are. Many, when they are rescued, are completely unbalanced and in a pitiable state.

There is nothing unusual about going astray. If such a situation is new to you, the best thing to do is to sit down, let your muscles go as comforably slack as possible, and begin thinking things over calmly. It will usually help if you go about your reasoning logically. A simple way to start is by asking yourself what's the trouble. That's easy. You don't know where you are in relation to where you want to go. In the vernacular, you're lost.

Once you've accepted that fact, ask yourself another question. So what is the worst that can happen to you? Well, you can starve. Yes, but on the other hand if a man doesn't unnecessarily exhaust himself, he can go for weeks without food. Besides, in a pinch, even the inner bark of such very common trees as birch, poplar, and the numerous evergreens will furnish nourishment. All cacti are good to eat. In the Arctic, all vegetation is edible except for one species of mushroom, although you'll want to soak the bitterness out of some of the lichens. All freshwater fish on this continent are edible, and so are all birds and all animals.

You probably won't starve then, but what about wild beasts? No wild animal in all North America—with the exception of the polar bear and the occasional grizzly—is dangerous to a man who does not provoke it.

What next? Well, you're expected back by nightfall, and you don't want to worry anyone. Of course, you don't want to worry anyone. That's one reason you're not going to blunder along inanely and maybe get into real trouble. If worst comes to worst, you can build a fire and sleep safely right here. It'll be a lot better to take care of yourself and let those who are waiting for you be a little anxious for a few hours, than to really give them something to worry about.

So that much is settled. If there is an experienced woodsman in your camp, you can take it easy right where you are. He will find you without any particular difficulty by at least the next morning. But if you start moving around, that can be another matter entirely. You may roam right out of the area of search. So why not select a cheerful spot nearby? Collect a lot of dry firewood, and go about preparing yourself an overnight bivouac. When viewed from retrospect, as a matter of fact, it'll probably be the high point of your trip.

If you are in the wilderness with a party, the sensible thing to do is to agree among yourselves beforehand exactly how you all are going to proceed in any such emergencies. This is no more than a fundamental precaution. Even the most experienced woodsman can have an accident that will immobilize him and make help necessary. Just to mention one possibility, a branch from' a dead tree might fall and break a leg.

SIGNALING FOR HELP

Such an understanding may include the agreement that anyone lost or otherwise in distress shall fire, on the hour, three shots that are evenly spaced about ten seconds apart. Fired at appreciable intervals in this way, and on the hour, these would patently be distress shots and not merely casual shooting at an animal. Furthermore, anyone alerted by hearing the first shot or the second would have a good chance to determine the direction. Besides, if your companions suspect you may be lost, they will be listening for you on the hour.

They may answer you and they may not, depending upon your arrangements and on a number of other factors. It may be that for one reason or another, such as wind direction, they may not hear those particular shots at all. In any case, sit tight. If you move and your friends, hearing the shots, come to where the shots sounded from, they will not find you there.

Above all, do not try to travel during the night. That's plumb dangerous. Not only are you apt to go really astray, but there is a great danger of sticking a limb into your eye or falling over a bank in the dark.

You'll do a lot better to stay where you are, to repeat your shots each hour up to pitch dark if you can, and in the meantime to get enough dry wood together to keep up a hearty and warming fire during the night. If you are short on ammunition, the most auspicious time to signal is at dusk, when the wind usually quiets and when, if you are not already back in camp, your companions will be most likely to be listening for you.

There are numerous other ways of signaling, too—with fire or smoke, by flashing with a mirror or any other bright surface, by thumping a hollow log or dead tree, and by innumerable other procedures that'll suggest themselves if the situation demands.

GETTING OUT BY YOURSELF

If there's no woodsman back in camp, then it may be advisable for you to try to find your own way out. You should travel only during the daylight hours, however, unless there are grave reasons for you to do otherwise. On the desert, to cite one exception, you'd do better in hot weather to lie up in shade during the day, digging a narrow east-west slit for this purpose if necessary.

Whatever you do, you should proceed systematically. One way to commence is to sit down and smooth off a piece of ground on which you can scratch a map with a stick. In what direction did you start off from camp in the morning? That information, incidentally, should be exchanged daily between all members of the party. Also, if you start out alone, either from a solitary camp or from a parked automobile, it is not a bad idea to leave a message in some prominent place stating your probable whereabouts and the expected time of your return.

Now that you are making a map, put in every detail that you can remember. It's remarkable how many times a seemingly unanswerable situation will clear up completely once you start applying concrete logic to it. How long ago was it when you knew just where you were? If this was only an hour before, then you probably have not traveled more than a mile or so since that time. You therefore know within that distance just where your camp is.

Draw whatever you are sure of on the map. Is the camp on a river? If so, you will have a long boundary to shoot at. The river runs from west to east and your outfit is on the north shore? So you head south. Are you, by any chance, in a wooded area crisscrossed by country roads? Then traveling in any direction in a straight line will bring you out.

Helpful Signs of Civilization

Is there a hill nearby from where you may be able to see a telltale lake or mountain range? Perhaps an easily climbed pine will put you in a position to locate where you are. What about sounds? Automobile horns indicate roads; locomotive whistles, probable miles of track. Sounds of chopping carry far, and so does the bark of a dog. Perhaps you can see or smell smoke from a stove or campfire. Possibly you can glimpse some sort of light at night. If you spot the latter, watch and find out all you can about it, in most cases staying safely where you are and marking the direction so that you will be sure of it in the morning.

How to Travel in a Straight Line

When you realize you are lost, you are not apt to be very far out of the way. So in attempting to get back, be sure you keep oriented. You can head in a straight line, without sun or

GETTING MIXED UP

Despite high water and the other place, you will occasionally get mixed up for a time. A little thought and common sense, however, will usually straighten you out. I can recall a dozen instances where I got messed up, all due to my own carelessness. Here is one of those instances.

It was in heavily wooded lake country. The day was clouded over. I had a fair map of the region. I arrived at the point marked "1," intending to go to the lake at the top of the map along the route shown by the dotted line.

It was obvious that all I had to do was to fight my way for a hundred yards through the alder swamps, and then around Hill A with the slope dropping off to my right, until I struck the lake. It was all so obvious that I paid no attention to my compass, intending to be guided by the contour of the hill. Except for the slope, the place was so wooded you could not see for any distance.

I crossed the thick alder swamp, but there was where I made my mistake. Without realizing it, I got turned too much to my left in the swamp. When I came out onto firm ground, there was the gentle slope slanting off to my right. I followed around as shown by the dash line, still not looking at my compass. I reached the first question mark. No lake! So I climbed up on top of Hill B to the second question mark. Still no lake!

Where was I, and what had I done? So for the first time I got out my compass, and then it was obvious that I had climbed around to the left. It was also perfectly obvious that if I steered south I would strike the little river and be able to follow it up to the lake. Which I did—T. W.

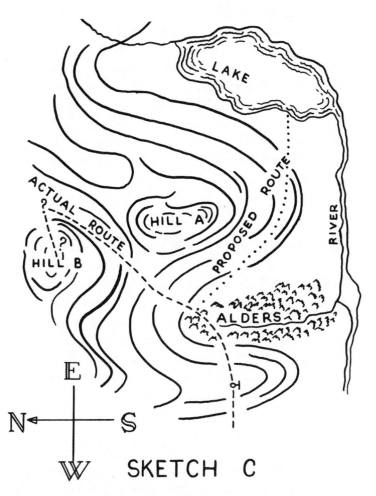

SKETCH C

If you do get mixed up, a little thought and common sense will usually be enough to straighten you out.

compass, by keeping two objects such as trees always lined up ahead of you. Before you reach the nearer of these, select another that maintains the direction. Or you can travel in a generally straight course, picking the easiest route and averaging the changes of direction. The latter technique, although usually preferable and in some terrain absolutely necessary, requires much closer attention.

If you have the slightest doubt about what you are doing, carefully blaze or otherwise spot your way as you proceed. You will then be able to get back to where you started, and from that center you will be able to try another route. Furthermore, such markings may very well help your friends to find you. If someone may be searching for you, don't ever quit a camp without leaving information about where you're heading.

What About Following Streams?

The advice is often repeated that when anyone seems hopelessly turned around, all he has to do is follow a brook or river downhill. This, it has been said many times, will lead one to civilization sooner or later. The theory sometimes even takes swamps into consideration and recommends that one skirt these on their higher sides. Less prudently, it occasionally adds that if you can't find running water to follow, you have a good chance of locating it by climbing down into a canyon or ravine.

The whole idea of lost men heading along streams, however reasonable it may sound to someone who has never been in real wilderness, is actually impractical in the extreme. You might travel down some rivers for as many days and weeks as you could keep going, and you would end up even farther from human habitation. Such a route, furthermore, would almost surely lead you through the roughest and thickest sort of going—if not into valleys and muskegs that are dangerously impassable—or you might very well come to a tributary river you could not ford.

Using a Road to Point the Way

If you know of a well-defined road or a large lake with settlements on it that lies in a certain direction, even though it is a couple of days away, you might head for this as a last resort. For instance, if you are about twenty-five miles west of the Alaska Highway, you could travel generally east with the assurance that if you keep going you'll surely come to it.

But any time you are really lost and happen upon something such as a power line or a telephone wire strung through the woods, do not pass it by on the grounds that you may have some other sign of habitation in your mind. If you come to a road, do not cross it and continue on into more wilderness just because it does not seem to be the one you're looking for.

Such a precaution would seem, at first glance, so elementary as not to merit mentioning. But even in Alaska Highway country—where if one passes this thoroughfare, he will in some cases not encounter another though he proceed to the Pacific Ocean, Hudson Bay, or the Arctic Ocean—the tracks of some lost men have showed that they crossed this unmistakable wilderness turnpike two and three times and yet plunged right back into the bush.

Trial-and-Error Method

Whenever you go into strange country, be sure to keep a mind map of your whereabouts. This is a great deal easier than it sounds. It gets to be second nature with just a little practice.

MESSED UP WORSE

When big wet flakes began tumbling thick among the lodgepole pines the first winter I was lucky enough to stay in the sub-Arctic forest, I still needed a well-larded bear.

Fifteen minutes from the gleaming newness of my log cabin, I picked up a trapper's trail heading true north along an old survey line.

Although this trail hadn't been cut out for a couple of years, travel over it was far easier than in the bush. Besides, it slanted up a series of benches where bears had been working on bushes to which a few saskatoons still clung. Sure enough, I picked up a fresh track and had a packload of plump young bruin back on the trail by 10:00 A.M.

The snow had stopped by then. The sun was bright on its thinness, and a dry warm chinook wind was feathering flakes from the trees. It was too fine a day to head back so soon. So I kept following the trail, which continued north, for the first hour and a half through a jackpot left by fire. At 12:15, it doubled back downhill somewhere toward a swamp.

I decided to keep up on what was now a high poplar flat. This I did, continuing north at the same pace, with my shadow generally straight ahead of me but a trifle on the left, until I cut a brook at 1:00 P.M. Here I boiled the kettle for half an hour. The chinook was really whipping through the open country by then.

I'd been figuring on following my tracks easily back to the trail, ambling leisurely along to my loaded pack, and being at the cabin by dark.

No snow! Now what? Should I head back due south

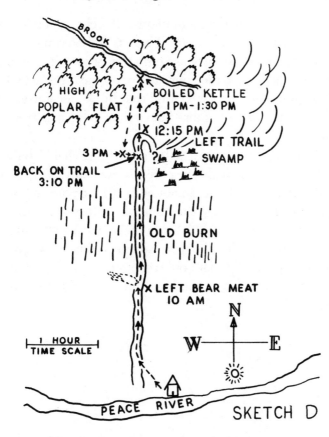

BROOK

HIGH POPLAR FLAT

BOILED KETTLE
1 PM - 1:30 PM

X 12:15 PM

LEFT TRAIL

3 PM →X→X

SWAMP

BACK ON TRAIL
3:10 PM

OLD BURN

X LEFT BEAR MEAT
10 AM

1 HOUR
TIME SCALE

N
W   E

PEACE RIVER

SKETCH D

and try to hit the north-south trail on the nose? Pretty slim chance! Should I travel south one hour at the same pace and then start zig-zagging southeast and south-west, extending these lines until I crossed the trail? Too long!

What I finally did was head south-southwest, where the walking seemed better than on the other slant, for an hour and a half at the speed I'd been traveling all day. I was then sure that the trapper's trail lay a few minutes east of me. Which it did.—B. A.

But suppose, in the excitement of the chase, you forget to keep such a map up to date? There is still nothing to worry about. Again you simply use common sense. Sit down and draw a rough map from your memory up to the point where, half an hour ago, you wounded that buck and started after him. You are now not more than a mile and a half from that point.

Take a course, say north, for a mile and a half. You won't be able to use time in this instance, for you are going to mark your route. Then if you do not come to the place where the buck was shot, return to the point of confusion. From there, set off on another line which you also blaze. Pretty soon, one of these radii will take you near enough to where you wounded your deer that you'll recognize just where you are. Never thereafter need you fear that you will get lost in any country.

15. All About Maps

A good map of the wilderness you visit can be of enormous help. It may well save you a lot of time and unnecessary work, enable you to plan your vacation better, and keep you from getting mixed up. In the faint forest flavor of its projections, relief-indicating shades, and intriguing keys lies the power to make an excursion more interesting and more challenging.

There is now scarcely a region in North America above the yellow deserts and the brown waters of the Mexican border that is not accurately mapped. This does not mean that every inch of North America has been thoroughly explored and that no longer are there blank spaces. Included among the primitive expanses, where your foot can still make the first human print, are those vast surfaces that have been mapped by aerial photography only, many after World War II pointed up the wide gaps in the map systems of the United States and Canada.

All aerial charts are extremely accurate insofar as the features depicted are concerned. However, the intimate details which would not show from the air are lacking. Such characteristics as rapids, trails, portages, wooded and open ground, and burns are often missing. Hills, mountains, and ravines many times do not stand out on aerial maps.

It used to be that we had to start out and tell the uninitiated how to read a map. But with the almost universal use of automobile road maps, that time is past. Nearly everyone now has a certain basic understanding of cartography.

Orienting a Map

The first thing to do when reading a map in the field is, of course, to orient it. Almost all are drawn so that true north is at the top. When this is not the case, the map is usually so marked. Very often on maps showing comparatively small areas, magnetic north—where, in that particular tract, your compass needle will point—is also indicated.

When your map is turned so that its north is in line with actual north, it will show the direction from where you are standing to every feature on it. From where you are, for example, a lake appears on the map about five miles away in a northwesterly direction. If you travel northwest for five miles, you will reach that lake. Conversely, if you are at the lake and your camp is at a junction of two streams drawn on the map, orient your map, lay a twig on it between where it shows the lake and the camp location, and that twig will point directly toward your outfit.

Where to Get Maps

The finest maps of the United States and Alaska are those produced by the U.S. Geological Survey. These are published in quadrangles which, at a scale of one inch to one mile, usually cover fifteen minutes of latitude and longitude. Such a sheet averages seventeen by twenty-one inches. Many of the more recent quads are scaled at one inch to a half-mile, embracing seven-and-one-half minutes of latitude and longitude.

Each quad sheet is designated by the name of some town or prominent object included in it. Maps covering areas in the states east of the Mississippi River are procurable from the U.S. Geological Survey, 18 and F Streets N.W., Washington, D.C. 20242. For states west of that river, including Louisiana and Minnesota, you will be able to obtain maps from the U.S. Geological Survey, Federal Building, Denver, Colorado 80225.

Write first for a free index sheet of the state in which you're interested. These detail the available quadrangles. When you order the individual maps you need, enclose the price for each by check or money order payable to the Geological Survey. Stamps are not accepted.

The back of every map shows the conventional signs and how to interpret any contours that indicate height, shape, and slope of hills and mountains. An arrow shows the compass declination. These maps are extremely accurate, but some were made years ago and may not depict recent roads, trails, and new small towns. So you'd better get an ordinary automobile road map, available without charge from gasoline dealers, to use with the quad.

Colored three-dimensional maps of many of the national parks, monuments, and historical sites are published and sold by the National Park Service, 15 and C Streets, Wahington, D.C. 20240. They are of great value to anyone interested in the natural features, geology, and history of the area and to those planning hiking or pack trips. Prices vary. Write for the free checklist.

The topographic maps—which describe the earth's surface by contour lines and in a few instances by shaded relief—show mountains, hills, valleys, passes, glaciers, trails, lakes, ponds, streams, springs, sand dunes, cliff dwellings, ruins, buildings, and other natural and man-made features. They also indicate the boundaries of the national parks and other areas of the National Park System.

Sectional maps are obtainable from the Superintendent of Documents, U.S. Government Printing Office, Washington, D.C. 20402.

For Canadian maps, write to the Map Distribution Office, Department of Mines and Technical Surveys, Ottawa, Ontario. Give the exact location or the latitude and longitude limits for which you wish maps, and ask for the price of the best ones available. Many of these are based on recent air photographs and are absolutely accurate, although they do not always show features that are not visible from a plane. In wilderness areas everwhere in the world, it's generally a sound idea to have a dependable warden, ranger, prospector, trapper, or local sportsman check trails, portages, and the like on your map before you take to the bush.

Canadian maps may also be procured, without charge, from the various tourist bureaus which are located in the capital cities of the various provinces. One central office to contact for free maps and detailed information is the Government Travel Bureau in Ottawa, Ontario.

As a rule, the best maps of other countries are those published by the National Geographic Society, 1145 17th Street N.W., Washington, D.C. 20036. A government source for Mexican maps, which will supply information about these upon your written request, is Direccion de Geografia y Meteorologia, Tacubaya, D.F., Mexico

Drawing Your Own Map

You are making a long journey through strange country by knapsack, with a pack train, or in a canoe. You are going to be gone many days, weeks perhaps, and possibly even months. You want to be able to find your way back. Or perhaps you wish a record of where you are going. Or it may be that you are aiming to come out at some particular point at the end of your trip. You may even be planning to do a little of the occasionally very profitable sort of prospecting we'll consider in a moment. In case a later assay indicates you've turned up something rich, you'll want to know exactly where you located those particular samples.

Over such an extended trip, it is obvious that you will not care to rely on a mind map. So why not draw one as you go along? No matter how unhandy you are with pencil or pen, you will be able to make a map that is plenty good enough to refresh your memory and to keep you straight as to general direction and distance. At the conclusion, you might like to burn a nostalgic copy into leather made from some trophy animal you secure along the way.

You can draw your map on any piece of paper. We have found convenient and inexpensive loose-leaf notebooks small enough to fit neatly somewhere about the person.

One of us has a little bundle of these whose pages recall a stray odor, brush of breeze, animal call, the resiliency of juniper with its pleasantly woodsy blue berries, and many other transient pleasures. A cool cedar swamp where deer can be secured at mid-day. A railroad bridge in the midst of spruce woods where we unloaded our canoe and outfit at midnight from a stuffy baggage car and were off down an uninhabited wilderness river in the misty dawn. A northern slope where a black bear hibernates. A stream where a grizzly was pouncing on flashing trout. The way a line of moose meadows are strung together like a giant necklace. A desert cave near the brook-sized Rio Grande in the shadow of the Sangre de Cristo Mountains.

Distances on your map should bear as close a relationship to distances on the ground as you can reasonably manage. We suggest that your drawing be scaled at a half-inch to every mile. You can then usually get a day's journey all on one sheet.

Draw, first of all, an arrow on the paper to indicate north, referring to your compass. Every time you sketch in any feature or route, you orient your paper; that is, you turn it until the arrow points north. If your journey for the day is to be in a westerly direction, start your draft at the east or right edge of the paper so as to get it all on the sheet.

MAPPING A PACK-TRAIN TRIP

If you are traveling by pack train, the map shown in Sketch E is the type you might draw. You start out from your one-night camp at dawn and travel southwest down a fairly steep hill for half an hour. On such a slope and a fair trail, your horses will not average over two and one-half miles per hour. So you draw, toward the southwest, a dotted line one and one-fourth inches long to indicate that portion of your trip.

At that point you come out into a valley extending westward, with high mountains on each side and a little stream glittering through its middle toward the rising sun. To the south is a high mountain with a peculiar summit. This you estimate to be about two miles from the creek which divides the valley. On the margin of your paper, you draw

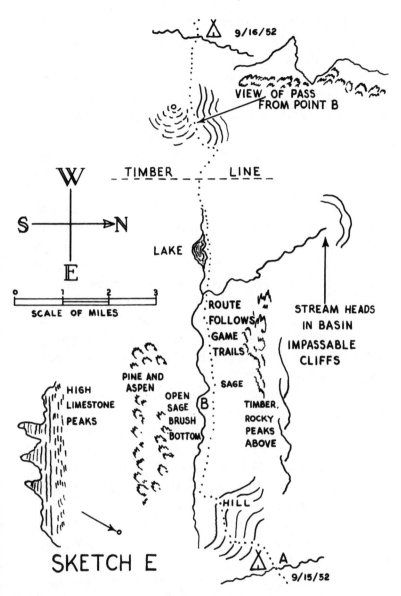

9/16/52

VIEW OF PASS
FROM POINT B

TIMBER — — LINE

W

S ➤N

E

SCALE OF MILES
0   1   2   3

LAKE

ROUTE
FOLLOWS
GAME
TRAILS

STREAM HEADS
IN BASIN

IMPASSABLE
CLIFFS

SAGE

HIGH
LIMESTONE
PEAKS

PINE AND
ASPEN

OPEN
SAGE
BRUSH
BOTTOM

B

TIMBER,
ROCKY
PEAKS
ABOVE

HILL

SKETCH E

A
9/15/52

If you draw a map of each daily route on a pack-train trip,
at journey's end you will have an accurate chart of the
entire trip.

an outline of this mountain so that when you come to it on your return, you'll know exactly where to swing northeast to catch the hill trail down which you just now have dusted.

You ride up the broad open valley with your shadow almost straight ahead of you. The slope up the creek is a gentle one, and the animals in your string nip occasionally at clumps of grass. You are following a succession of game trails. On such going, your pack train will probably make about three and one-half miles an hour, and so you time yourself accordingly.

At the head of the depression, there appears to be a pass through the snow-coned range you hope to pierce. So about halfway along, you pause for a couple of minutes and sketch a rough outline of the way that pass, if such it is, looks from the center of the valley. Pretty soon the creek heads up in a little lake which you draw in to scale. It took you a little less than an hour and a half to reach this lake from where you started up the vale. Therefore, you have traveled about five miles in this stretch, and you mark it with a dotted line two and one-half inches long.

After you go around the lake, the way becomes steeper and rougher. Your cayuses are making only a couple of miles an hour now. It takes nearly sixty minutes to reach the summit of the pass, so you note that in a dotted line one inch long. About a mile further along, you drop down into the timber beside a little creek where there is good grazing. You unpack your animals, hobble them, bell your saddle mare, which is the leader, and make your camp for the night. Adding this information on your paper, you conclude your charting for today.

Now on this sheet you have a pretty good little map. It is not as fine a one as a topographical engineer would make, but it is plenty accurate enough to enable someone else to follow your trail or to make certain that you will be able to return this way next month or next year. If your total journey is to be for twelve days, you will end up with a dozen of these sheets. Joined together with the north arrows all pointing in the same direction, these will make a composite map of a probably unforgettable journey.

MAPPING PROSPECTING FINDS

The demand for certain raw materials being what it is these days, you might like to do a little prospecting along the route. The more you know about this subject, the more you'll enjoy yourself, but it is not necessary even to be able to distinguish between serpentine and schist to have a reasonable chance of making a rich strike.

Fording a stream while on a pack-train trip.

When you see an unusual ledge or outcrop, knock off a sample. Number it. On the map you are keeping enter a corresponding number. Don't bother too much with loose rocks. Because of glacial and stream action, these may be thousands of miles from their source. It is sometimes possible to trace drift back up a river, then up a certain stream, and finally along a short tributary to the mother lode. But some of our acquaintances have spent entire lifetimes trying to do just that. So stick mostly to interesting formations that are in place.

Not far from where you live, there is some governmental or educational group that will give you at least a preliminary report on your samples without cost. Perhaps you can mail in the samples. If something does turn out to be promising, you can tell by looking at your map exactly where to relocate it.

Unless you are going in for gravel punching in a big way, you can handle all the panning you need to do for samples with a frypan burned free of grease. Fill this with gravel and sand generally from spots where heavy small materials, borne by water, might be expected to accumulate: in back of large boulders, on the upstream portions of bars, and, especially, down close to bedrock and in any crevices therein.

Panning merely capitalizes on the tendency of heavy particles, such as gold, to concentrate at the bottom. Large stones and such you pick out. Filling the pan with water, you break up any lumps of dirt and such by hand. You rotate the vessel briskly under water which, in dry desert washes, may be in a big kettle. (In this case, the handle of the frypan will have been removed.) Keep shoving the coarser stuff out. When you've sized down pretty well, tilt the receptacle a bit and rotate it easily so as to bunch any heavy minerals on the bottom. Then raise the pan until the tilted lip is just beneath the surface. Rotate and dip a few times, brushing off the lighter top materials.

Depending on where you're washing, pretty soon you should be down to maybe a damp patch of black sand that's largely iron oxide. Swirl this about in a little water, looking for colors. Any small particles of gold remaining after washing may be little more than specks, but enough of them will add up to the pokes of dust that can rock empires.

Copper or iron pyrites, known as fool's gold, are bright only in light and shatter easily. Muscovite, seen in flakes of brassy-looking mica—containing aluminum, silicon, oxygen, and either hydrogen or potassium—will break up readily between your fingernails. Gold, often accompanied by platinum and silver, gleams yellow even in dark canyon shadows, although it is usually dull-colored.

CHARTING A CANOE JOURNEY

Now let's take another kind of country—the lake and river expanses of the Northeast through which, as indicated by Sketch F, you and a companion are gliding with a canoe. You will need, first of all, some kind of a time-distance schedule. This you should make yourself by paddling over a measured mile or a longer course, for a great many factors influence the speed you can maintain in a canoe: how strong and skillful you are with the paddle; the physical aspects of your loaded craft; wind direction; type of water; current; and a dozen other factors.

Under some of these conditions, as when your efforts are added to the smooth flow of a river, you'll find you will make six miles an hour. When you have to pole and occasionally line the craft up through bad water, it may take you

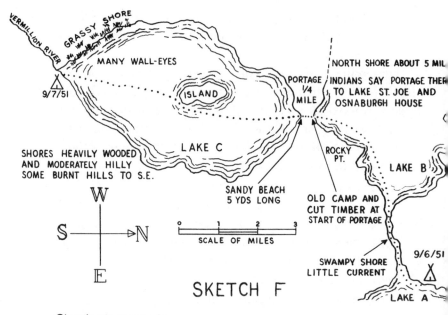

Charting a canoe journey.

all morning to cover one-half that distance. All these aspects you must take into consideration in setting down your distances on the map.

You make this map just as you did the one when your rifle in its saddle scabbard bulged under your knee. If there is any feature about which you are not sure, show it in dashes rather than with a solid line. As you came out of the inlet between Lake A and Lake B, for example, you saw two points of land against the north shore of the latter. You could not see up into what looked like a bay, however. As a matter of fact, the second mass of land may well have been an island. So you simply show the dashed line extending a little way into the opening between the first and second promontories.

Almost every lake in the canoe country of North America has old Indian portages connecting it with other lakes. Many a river has similar carries around rapids. Some of these are marked by lob-sticks, prominent trees from which a number of upper branches have been conspicuously lopped. The beginnings of others are so obscure that it is difficult for even an experienced bushman to find them. There may be an old tea-stick, or grass bent down, or a scraped log or rock. It is important that you note the start and the end of such portages as accurately and definitely as possible on your map, detailing particularly any salient features by which they may be distinguished, as suggested in Sketch F.

Often in strange country you may be able to locate other lakes, and the portages between, by ascending a hill from which you can get an extended view. Where two such bodies of water come closest together is where you'll usually find a carry, even though this may be an old Indian track that has not been used for fifty years. Evidences still remain of the portage Alexander Mackenzie made past the upper waters of Rocky Mountain Canyon when, in 1793, he led up the Peace the first party ever to cross the North American continent north of Mexico. Others had been trying to accomplish this feat ever since Columbus happened upon the New World 301 years before.

How to Find Lake Outlets

When you are trying to follow a string of lakes, or to make your way along a river which is continually expanding into small and large stillnesses, as big streams often do in Canada, it is sometimes exceedingly difficult to find where the outlet of one body of water leads into the next. It may be at the head of any one of a half dozen bays.

Near such an outlet or inlet there is usually a little current which will cause the water grass to bend over in the direction of the flow. You'll sometimes see an old bushman trying to detect such motion by dropping some bannock crumbs overboard and watching their action. There are such telltale matters, too, as gulls on the watch for feed congregating near such passages, while for some the dip of hills holds a significant story.

16. The Lowdown on Canoes

There's an exhilaration, a rhythm, and a fierce clean freeness to canoeing in the wild places that takes it out of the realm of other sports. Nothing brings you more alert. Every muscle responds immediately, with both power and delicacy, to the swiftly shifting demands of balance and steerage. You poise almost quivering with restrained energy, studying which racing bulge of water to ride around an onrushing boulder. Then you're driving your blade with fast, hefty jabs. You're fighting to swing the stern free of a suddenly chortling current that hungers to heave the craft broadside up against a froth-dampened projection and there snap it in two.

With a sudden lift and plunge, you're past. Instantly you're fairly met with another challenge to every last iota of your strength, judgment, and skill—and another, and still another. You eye ahead, brace yourself, and turn your instantaneous decisions into exultant action amid the rush and hiss of wind and contesting water.

Then you're through the last of this intoxicating craziness. The stream widens into a deep gentleness. It is so abruptly quiet that when your paddle scrapes a gunwale the brief clatter seems a desecration, although you know the current is merely bunching behind another rock-pierced narrowness somewhere ahead. You see the perfect birch under which to spread your eiderdown. Your legs quiver a little when you step ashore. You draw in a deep breath. You're ten feet tall.

We've only experienced one other sensation remotely comparable to the excitement and satisfaction you win by shooting a primitive river under your own steam. That's feeling the smooth, muscular speed of your own favorite saddle horse rippling beneath you along an open ridge trail as, in sheer exuberance after a successful day's hunt, you're racing campward in the first cool dampness of a wilderness evening.

The Best Canoe Country

Northen America east of the Mississippi embraces the finest canoe country in the world. Maine and adjoining portions of Canada, the Adirondacks in New York, and Wisconsin afford opportunities for long and short cruises through interesting silences. There are many small eastern rivers that tinkle and gurgle across lowlands into the Atlantic, or the Mississippi, traversing regions where one can usually camp freely, and which provide good fishing and sometimes good enough hunting as well.

The most superb canoe stronghold of all lies in northern Minnesota and in northern and western Ontario and Quebec. In these latter regions you find a practically unspoiled wilderness with almost as much water as land, and such myriads of small lakes that it is literally possible on any given day to paddle your little craft toward any point of the compass.

All this land has been Indian canoe country for hundreds of generations. Wherever there is an obstacle to water travel, you will usually find a portage, a trail or easy way through or around. In the North we have seen portages which are worn a foot deep in the soil and where the very rocks have been polished by thousands of moccasins.

The only real practical craft for the sportsman who travels such waters is the canoe. This can be easily portaged around rapids, past thunderous falls, and between lakes—on one man's shoulders, if need be. In a canoe, game can be noiselessly approached. Because the canoe is made to be handled with its occupants facing forward, it is the only satisfactory craft for running the usual rapids and for ascending swift streams. It can be paddled. It can be poled. It can be lined. You can wade it, too, handling it where waters momentarily deepen by swimming with one hand on the stern.

CONTINENTAL NORTHWEST

Throughout the great continental Northwest, large rivers slant hundreds and sometimes thousands of miles through splendid and almost virgin country. Most of these rivers can be ascended a long way, almost to their sources, in canoes.

In many regions, because of the tremendous distance to be covered, long narrow wooden boats capable of carrying barrels of gas in addition to heavy outfits are more commonly used. Some of these are powered by inboard motors, often salvaged from some truck or automobile that has been finally put out of commission by the primitive roads of the area. Others are kicked along by big outboard motors, sometimes operated from an elevated seat in back.

By fall, there is little game along these streams except for occasional moose, bear, and a few deer. Prospectors licensed to keep themselves in meat do all right in spring and summer, however. In the mountains, they sometimes even catch up to a swimming goat.

Trophy hunters travel these rivers until they are as near as they can get to good hunting range. They then backpack into the mountain habitats of sheep, goat, caribou, moose, and grizzly. Such a trip is really an expedition, to be planned months in advance and to be undertaken only by experienced and strong outdoorsmen.

Choosing a Canoe to Suit Your Needs

The longest canoe journey I have made was for seventy-five days, about half of which were travel days, through the wilderness of northern Ontario. Our seventeen-foot canvas

The turbulent Peace River in front of the Angiers' cabin.

canoe weighed eighty pounds and our outfit, at the start, just about 400 pounds more. Of course, the weight of the latter diminished daily as grub was consumed. On a number of wilderness trips about half that long, Brad has taken everything he wanted in a fifteen-footer weighing just short of sixty pounds dry. He kept its sleek cedar interior and canvas covering freshly varnished and painted to reduce the absorption of heft-increasing moisture.

Today, the Grumman aluminum alloy canoes have it over other types in almost every way, although you'll probably want to subdue the glare with a dead-grass shade of paint, and to include the available rubber gunwale guards for both stern and bow paddlers in the interest of silence.

The size of the canoe to be chosen depends largely on the bulk and weight to be carried, on the skill and huskiness of the occupants, and on whether many large lakes must be negotiated. The particular craft must not be loaded so heavily that it will be sluggish, hard to turn, or slow to respond to paddle. It should lift over large swells with characteristic leaflike buoyancy rather than plough through with a resultant shipping of water. There must be sufficient freeboard so that waves encountered on fairly windy days will not swamp the craft.

No canoe can be expected to weather a serious storm on a large body of water. During a squall, simply go ashore and wait for a calmer spell. But the canoe should not be laden so heavily that it will be unsafe in the chop and waves of an ordinary blow.

Canoe Repair Kits

With an aluminum craft, it is wise to include one of the special kits containing patches, sealing compound, and rivets. Minor punctures can usually be temporarily repaired with cold solder, marine glue, or even a strip of ordinary waterproof adhesive tape from your medicine kit. With a canvas canoe, pack along one of the waterproof glues, some heavy canvas, a can of copper tacks, some white lead, and maybe an old spoon and brush. We've also done pretty well in a pinch by using spruce pitch, melted along with a candle stub, in which to soak and cement on a strip of fabric requisitioned from the flap of a duffel bag.

Portaging the Canoe

The average canvas canoe suitable for wilderness travel—and still the favorite in Canada—will weigh about eighty pounds, and the aluminum craft somewhat less. It is not nearly as difficult to take one of these canoes over portage as anyone who has not tried it might expect, particularly as the load balances itself on your shoulders and presses straight down.

CARRYING YOKES

Almost invaribly the experienced canoeist uses his two paddles to form the carrying yoke. These are lashed with something such as cod line or babiche between the center thwart and front seat, blades to the former and handles to the latter. The three-inch-wide part of the upper portion of the blade should come just in front of the thwart. The distance between two blades should be such that they will lie comfortably on the shoulders when the back of the neck is resting slightly against the thwart.

A well-made canoe should nearly balance on the center thwart, being just a trifle heavier toward the stern. Then,

An Indian repairs his homemade canoe.

when your head and shoulders are in place and, reaching a little ahead, you grasp each gunwale and pull down slightly to balance the boat, its bow will ride about six feet above the ground. This clearance will enable you to choose your footing and to steer the craft past trees and other obstacles.

TAKING UP THE LOAD

There are several ways to get a canoe up on your shoulders. Until you get the knack, any of these can strain you, especially when you're still soft from city living. Better get an experienced canoeman to coach you, and don't attempt anything beyond your strength. The easiest and safest method is to turn the canoe over. While your companion raises the bow at arm's height above his head, step under, place your head between the paddles and the back of your neck against the thwart, and lift. For a carry of more than fifty yards or so, some padding for the shoulders will be desirable.

Loading the Canoe

A canoe should be loaded only when it is afloat or nearly so. The weight, preferably centered as low as possible, should be so distributed that when both men step in, the canoe will ride just noticeably deeper at stern than at bow. It should always be so trimmed, of course, that the side balance is absolutely central.

PROTECTING GEAR FROM DUNKINGS

A good precaution in some water is to lay a light tarp amidships and to stow all but the heaviest articles in this. Finish by drawing the canvas up around the thus enclosed outfit and lashing it as securely closed as possible. The ax can be shoved within easy reach under these lashings and the strap of its sheath buckled over one or more lashings as an extra safety measure.

Do not tie or otherwise attach this bundle to the canoe. Anything particularly cumbersome and heavy, like bags of canned goods (their contents identified by scratches in case the labels are soaked off) should be laid by itself directly on the bottom of the craft and the tarp-wrapped essentials packed atop them. Then if you happen to have a wreck, the essentials will float and you'll have an excellent chance of recovering them with contents intact and dry. This is particularly true if the highly buoyant sleeping bags are included within the tarp. In any event, the canoe can be loaded much more compactly if these are so folded before being rolled that they can be wedged from side to side instead of being stowed lengthwise.

There is another angle to sleeping robes that may be well to keep in mind. Those with down, fresh kapok, and similar fillers make good life preservers to grab in an emergency, especially if you have a stout strap or thong on them where you can grasp it in a hurry. A lot of bushmen keep their sleeping bags handy for this reason, often using them for a seat or for a pad on which to kneel while paddling. In a small canoe, however, an inexpensive life preserver cushion will serve the same purpose a lot more conveniently.

On a canoe trip it is imperative to have a well-devised system of packing and handling your outfit; careful organization is rewarded by having more time to enjoy your camp.

RIFLE PROTECTION

All our wilderness rifles have slings attached with quickly detachable swivels. In rough water, it is easy to unsnap one swivel, pass the sling under a thwart of the canoe, and snap the swivel on again. Then if we have an upset, and we've both experienced them, we do not lose a rifle.

Because of the dampness encountered during a canoe trip, it's a good idea to bring along a waterproof gun case. A plain plastic cover that weighs scarcely anything, and which folds as small as a handkerchief, will protect the rifle from rain. Used in camp, it will keep off the night dew which often wets weapons as badly as if they had been out in a storm. A wet or warped stock can entirely change the zero setting of your rifle.

In camp, cut two short forked stakes, drive them in the ground alongside your bed, and lay the encased rifle across them. If you happen to be out without a case in misty or frosty weather, a dry place to cache the rifle is between a full-length air or foam mattress and a ninety-by-ninety sleeping robe. If you place the rifle near the edge away from the side you get in, it will remain well protected all night, and won't be in the way.

KEEPING HANDY THINGS HANDY

Anything you want to get during the day, such as lunch or a boiling kettle, tuck conveniently into a side space of the canoe. Cameras and fishing tackle should also be accessible. Tents and waterproofs should be on the outside of rolls and packs in case you have to make camp in a downpour. If you figure you are going to need your down jacket, wedge it up under the bow or stern deck where you can get at it easily.

The first individual across a portage should bring an ax in

case any cutting has to be done. The fellow whose job it is to tote the canoe should first go over a strange carry with a pack to become familiar with it. When he takes the canoe over, another packer should go along with him if possible.

If two campers can reduce their duffel to just three packs, each of which they can carry without undue effort, the work of portaging will be greatly simplified. They'll then have to make but two trips. Each will take a pack load on the first. On the second, one will bring a pack and help the other with the canoe where he can.

Whether you adopt these methods of packing and handling your outfit, or have the fun of devising a routine of your own, adhere to a system. Have a place for everything and everything in its place. It means less labor, delay, and confusion in traveling and in camp, and you have more time to devote to your chosen sport.

Such a system also removes most of the drudgery from portaging. It can even make a carry something to look forward to as a break in the monotony of paddling, an opportunity to stretch the legs, and in chilly weather a chance to get some welcome exercise—all provided there are no confounded bugs. Skeeters and black flies can turn a portage into something else again. But you'll soon forget any discomforts at the next glittering challenge of open water.

17. What to Expect on Pack Train Trips

Throughout the mountains and foothills of western North America, from the dusty mesquite of Mexico to the Arctic Circle, almost all the good big-game country is at least two or three days travel from the railroad or the nearest auto or wagon road. Outdoorsmen have to pack their outfits and supplies into these regions, and the most common method of transport is with pack animals.

Pack Horses' Memories: How Reliable?

Some years ago, I was hunting on the eastern slope of the Coast Range Mountains in British Columbia, and one afternoon I camped by a fine spring. I had with me a good pinto saddle mount named Chilly and a wise old pack horse called Loco. As was my custom, I chopped a saucer out of a fallen log and placed some salt and sugar in it for the horses. This both kept the horses around camp and made it easy to catch them.

Next morning I broke camp and went north for three miles through a flat covered thickly with jackpines. Mule deer had worn a game trail among the greenness of the conifers, and this dim path was the only easy way across the bench.

Neither I nor the horses had ever been in this country before. But two months later I came back from the opposite direction, wishing to camp at the same spring. There was now a foot of snow on the ground. The game trail was absolutely indistinguishable, and the jackpines looked unfamiliar in the heaviness of snow. I got off Chilly, put him in the lead, and drove the two horses ahead of me. Without hesitation, Chilly took that return trail for the three miles straight to the campsite, went up to the fallen log, nosed the snow off it, and started to lick.

This is not meant to imply that you can rely on a horse to keep you from getting lost, any more than you can on a dog, except in each animal's own neighborhood. Even there, the abilities of various horses in this respect differ markedly. Chinook, a sorrel mare one of us rides, all the time waits for an opportunity to circle very, very gradually. If you're just daydreaming along through the bush in cloudy weather, you're apt to glance around and find yourself heading back to camp. With the almost undectable aid of her nose, Chinook follows a back trail almost hoofprint for hoofprint when given her head.

On the other hand, the wife of one of us has a saddle mare that gets turned around as quickly as the greenest tenderfoot. In a way, this is a redeeming characteristic. The reluctance with which a lot of cayuses leave their home grounds becomes an exasperation at times. Copper, once you've trotted her into the bush and circled her around a few times, travels with equal enthusiasm in any direction. She's as anxious as the next mare to get back to the bundle of oats

Only with pack horses can you take an outfit adequate for extensive roaming into such superbly unspoiled country as this.

which she knows will be waiting. But even when night is nearing, if you just sit motionless in the saddle when approaching a reasonably familiar trail, about half the time Copper will quicken her pace along the wrong turning.

Daily Routine in a Pack Train

The prospective sheep-and-goat shooter who has not previously hunted with a pack train should understand certain details about the horse and his load, and some of the procedures of traveling, camping, and hunting. Keeping the horses in good condition is the primary essential.

You're already under canvas, let us assume. The party is going to break camp and travel on this day. At the first quickening of dawn, the wrangler starts out to find and drive in the animals which were turned loose the afternoon before to feed. Most of them, probably, have hobbles strapping their front legs together. The bells buckled around their necks will clang, bong, and peal the melody of their whereabouts.

When the wrangler drives the horses into camp, everyone on hand except the cook turns out to catch them, tie them to trees, and saddle them.

THE COOK

The cook, in the meantime, has piled out at dawn, although not with any bright song of joy. Because of various air currents put into motion by the blending of night with day, it's colder now than it was during total blackness. Maybe he deposits a dead old pine stump, saved for the purpose, in the center of the last fading embers of the campfire.

Tough country challenges the pack horses; keeping them in good condition is essential on a pack train trip.

This gives him a blaze like the light of a pressure lantern, and it also helps him to get some warmth into his fingers. Pretty soon he's thawed out enough to shove the coffee pot grumpily into the heat. He then begins banging pans around, a little more expressively than necessary.

One especially gregarious trail cook we know has a habit of carrying on a one-sided conversation, so provocative that anyone snoozing nearby is apt to hear himself joining in. Whereupon a grin spreads over this cook's face, for all he really wanted was company, and now he keeps exchanging remarks with such robust good humor that further sleep is impossible. The coffee smells too good, anyway, particularly when joined by the aromas of flippers and bacon.

Sometimes none of these devices work. Then the cook,

with a certain grim righteousness, sets about personally
arousing one and all in time for hot porridge, bacon, eggs,
flapjacks, fruit and your choice between steaming pots of
coffee and tea. A feminine member of the party he may call
the "just once" most trail cooks insist upon, by the simple
device of opening the valve of her air matress.

The cook then sees to it that everyone gets his lunch, in
many cases put up the night before. He washes and dries the
dishes. He packs the kitchen and the food panniers, making
sure that what he needs for the next meal is where he can get
at it first. He may then turn to with the others to roll up the
tents, so that when the wrangler gets back with the horses,
everything will be ready to be packed on them.

LOADING PACK AND SADDLE HORSES

There is no standard size for panniers. Most of them, the
best ones, measure on the outside about twenty-two inches
long, fifteen inches high, and nine inches deep from front to
back. Packers prefer the bottom-angled back so the pannier
will not stick out so much on the animal and bump into trees.
A pannier six inches wide is functional.

The top, bottom, and sides can be made of three-eighths
or half-inch waterproof plywood, and the ends of seven-
eighths-inch pine or spruce. To prevent mice or chipmunks
from getting at the contents, the pannier can be lined with
tin or with copper screening. Notches on the front edges are
made for the lash ropes—which secure the pannier on the
sawbuck saddle—to ride in. Hinges and fasteners can be
either metal or leather.

I have two of these panniers. One is for kitchen and
eating utensils. It will hold my nest of three aluminum
kettles, frypans, plates, cups, bowls, and cans of salt, sugar,

A bottom-angled back will keep the pannier from bumping into trees on narrow trails.

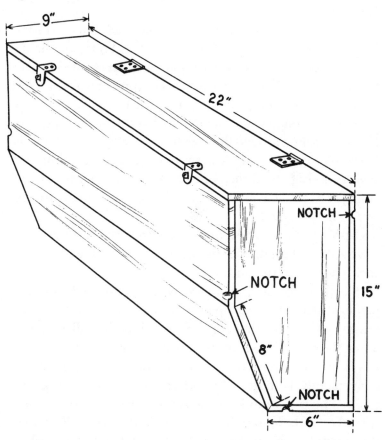

pepper, butter, and lard. The other takes my personal and photographic equipment. Tent, sleeping bag, air mattress, and a big wash and mixing pan go on top.

Various camp outfitters sell panniers, or kyacks as they're also called, made of fiberboard and plywood. You can also build them yourself, as most bushmen do. Some are made of the heaviest canvas. Especially picturesque, although not as practical as wooden varieties, are panniers made of tough untanned cowhide laced together with the hair outside.

An outfitter will usually assign one pack horse to each sportsman for carrying his personal outfit. Your rifle should go in a heavy leather scabbard slung on your saddle horse in the way you find handiest. Camera equipment is also usually stowed on the riding horse. So are your binoculars.

In open country, saddlebags are handy for this purpose. If you're sidling around through trees, anything breakable is better wrapped in your extra shirt or other such clothing and tied securely behind the pommel. Watch it, too, when you stop, for a lot of cayuses have a habit of occasionally rolling over when saddled.

Fishing rods can be a problem. Often, the best idea is to have a stout aluminum or fiber case for the rods and to trust their packing to the outfitter.

Sleeping bag and air mattress may be rolled in a tarpaulin about eight feet square, or in a small tent or shelter fabric, and tied with a rope. Such a bundle will measure about three feet by a foot and a half. Flat rather than round, it will be some seven or eight inches thick, and can thus be conveniently laid atop the saddle and panniers on a top pack. The pack cover of heavy waterproofed canvas, spread over the load before the hitch is thrown, will protect the equipment from rain and from snagging in the brush.

If you're on your own, stow the ax in its sheath where it will be both safe and readily accessible. On a pack horse, it can generally be shoved under the lashings, with the handle facing backwards and with the sheath strapped over a rope as an additional precaution against loss.

Many outfitters you'll travel with will furnish you with two panniers in which to carry extra clothing and other items for your individual use. Generally speaking, you place the most often wanted articles at the top. Use shirts and such to wrap breakables. Possessions such as binoculars and telescopes, which dampness can raise hob with, you tie securely within slightly inflated waterproof bags. We used to use the oilskin variety, but now lighter and far tighter plastic containers are cheaper and not as bulky.

Equal weights must, as nearly as possible, be placed in each pannier so that the two will balance on the animal. Desirable maximum weights vary. Fifty pounds if often the limit.

Immediately after breakfast, then, each sportsman packs his two panniers and bundles up his bedroll. He makes sure that he has everything on his person that he'll want during that day. He checks to see if his rifle, clothing, and camera are ready to secure on his saddle.

Two experienced men working together will pack a horse in about ten minutes when everything is at hand. From this, you can figure approximately how long it will take to get on the trail after the animals arrive. Every sportsman should learn how to pack. You can never tell when it may be necessary for you to lend a hand. Besides, one day you may want to get away on such a trip by yourself.

Anyone can learn to throw the necessary lashes and hitches—the diamond and one or two of the often ample simpler knots such as the half-diamond and the squaw—in two or three lessons provided he does a little practicing with a piece of string during spare moments.

A good woolen blanket or an adequate pad goes on first. This must be smooth and soft. Next comes a saddle that fits the individual animal. It should have breast and breech straps and double cinches. Before you tighten the cinches, put a finger under the front center of the blanket and lift it slightly along the spine. Sling on the panniers, secure them, lay what you're going to across or between them, and spread your pack cover in place. Then, with a strong half-inch rope braided to the ring of a canvas pack cinch, which at its other extremity has something such as a large wooden hook, bind down the entire load.

THE WRANGLER

When the outfit is ready to hit the trail, the lead rope of all but the front horse is tied to the pack of the one ahead with a knot that can instantly be jerked free if something

Two experienced men working together can pack a horse in about ten minutes when everything is at hand.

goes wrong. The wrangler holds the lead of the foremost animal and rides off.

Or—the horses are turned loose, the wrangler starts ahead, and the cook closes up behind. Occasionally a horse bolts out of line, and the rear man urges him back. This he does slowly and quietly, so as not to excite the string. Some days may be full of all kinds of trouble—spooked horses, turning packs, and snagged or bogged down animals. Little distance will then be covered. On other days we've traversed as much as a rousing thirty miles.

The wrangler is the man to say where the next camp shall be made. He is responsible for the horses, and he must stop where feed is good, where there's water, and where he can hold the animals reasonably close.

How to Rig a Saddle Horse

Usually, the sportsman and his guide will start off right after breakfast on their own horses, either to hunt or just to ride through the most interesting country. Often they'll arrive at the next camp after the train has pulled in, to find the shelters already pitched and the cook sour-faced again maybe because someone has had some jocose remark to make about the mulligan that is simmering. On some occasions, too, the sportsman will travel with the pack train, out front where he can spot game and keep out of the dust. In either event, he should see to the saddling of his own horse!

The natural tendency when saddling, especially with the heavier of the western jobs, is to heave the girth rings and stirrups too high. This causes them to bang noisily against such tender spots as leg joints and ribs. A lot of resultant shying and sidestepping can be avoided by swinging these

The competent saddle horse is not only a wonderful companion, but an excellent sentinel for game hunting.

just high enough to land easily on your mount's back where they'll slide down smoothly. You can then reach underneath and finish cinching without going around to the off side to straighten things up.

A lot of outdoorsmen planning trophy hunts in the West don't have much opportunity to familiarize themselves beforehand with horses or with the design and function of the riding gear characteristic to that part of the continent. This is unfortunate because the competent saddle horse is, in particular, a wonderful companion and an excellent sentinel as well. We've both shot considerable game whose presence was first sensed by our mounts. Once you become accustomed to hunting with a good horse, there's nothing else quite like it.

Maybe the following few hints which we have picked up from time to time, usually the hard way, will give you a little better idea of what lies ahead of you.

Mounting

When you're ready to get on, particularly if you and the horse are strangers, the main thing is to be in control. Horses differ. With a very few, you'll have to rein the head either in or around. Others begin to fret and sometimes to pitch if you're that heavy on bit. Mostly, a firm but light hold on the lines will be sufficient.

Unless you want to be bequeathed the deadest old plug in the remuda the next day out, don't like a lot of dudes, clamber up into the saddle and then yell for someone to hand you the ding-blasted reins.

Pack-Horse Trips for Two

There is no reason why two men reasonably accustomed to handling horses, camping, and traveling with a map should not take an extended pack horse trip by themselves. It means a lot of work, for if you hunt persistently during the day, you will have cooking, tackle repairs, and odd jobs to take care of sometimes late into the night. Horse wrangling, too, will frequently interfere with a planned stalk.

Two men can rent, or often more cheaply buy, four horses and live the life for months at a time. One pack horse will be able to carry all the outfit needed. The other, if you plan carefully, will have no trouble in handling enough food for a couple of men for a month. As for taking care of your horses, lone trappers and prospectors often travel with six or seven.

In many states and in some of the provinces of Canada, however, the law requires a nonresident hunter to be accompanied by a registered or licensed guide. Too, before outdoorsmen attempt such trips on their own, they should make sure that they are competent by experiments in country safely close to civilization. Generally speaking, furthermore, they must be of such a temperament that they will find as much satisfaction and delight in riding, packing, doing camp work, and attending to cooking, as in hunting and fishing.

18. How to Get Close to Game

When you leave camp for a day of big-game hunting, the chances are that you are carrying about ten cartridges in addition to those in your loaded rifle, along with a knife, a watch, a compass, a waterproof match box, a small tea pail maybe, and a lunch. A camera in its case may hang over a shoulder.

You may also have along binoculars to help you to determine, while there's still time to do something about it, if certain suspicious objects aren't game. Likely there will be other items bulging from your pockets: handkerchief, map, notebook, pencil, tiny first aid kit, exposure meter, extra film, sunglasses, small mirror, piece of cord, and carborundum stone.

A lot of hunters, if the weather is at all cold, start off in the chill of the morning in a heavy mackinaw. In addition, many so stuff their pockets and weigh down their belts that, particularly if they push through any tamarack with its shedding needles, they soon look and feel like an overloaded Christmas tree.

They puff, and grunt, and perspire along in a bulky jacket as they top hills and breast-thick bush. The straps of camera and glasses continually hang them up. The pull and strain of loaded clothing becomes more and more uncomfortable. The chances are that by now they would like to shed that coat, but they have nowhere to carry it.

All or most of this impedmenta is often desirable on a day's hunt. That particular system of carrying it, however, is unnecessarily handicapping and unduly out of date. I started out more than sixty years ago lugging my stuff more or less in this fashion until I noted that most of the world's most experienced hunters, except those accompanied by guides or gunbearers, toted such articles in a rucksack on their backs. I thereupon adopted this method and have adhered to it ever since.

Once you have carried a light rucksack for three or four days afield, you will never thereafter notice you have it with you. All discomfort is gone. Nothing dangles or catches. Your belt does not restrict you the way it did before. Your pockets do not bulge or press.

As you warm from exercise, off comes the jacket or extra shirt and into your rucksack it goes. If you stop to scan a promising slope or to enjoy lunch, or if you begin threading along a windy ridge, there is your extra clothing to put on again. You can get at everything quickly, and the rucksack is no burden at all.

Camp outfitters stock many models, but those rucksacks having two small pockets on the outside of the big central sack are most desirable, particularly if they have leather instead of web straps. Such models are usually made of a light waterproof duck cloth. If the color is too near that of a game animal, simply baste a red bandanna handkerchief over the outside when hunting in frequented forests.

My rucksacks have all been of this type, my present one being made of tanned moosehide of my own killing, and thong-sewed, but that is perhaps a pardonable affectation.

For ordinary one-day hunts, your pack and its contents should never weigh over ten pounds. Even when you anticipate the desirability of staying out from your base camp overnight, the pack need not weigh in excess of fifteen pounds. Such cargoes are scarcely felt after you have accustomed yourself to carrying a light load on your lower back. Packing of this sort is, indeed, not nearly so tiring as hiking in boots that weigh a pound more than your city shoes.

The Best Times to Hunt

Before we inventory the desirable contents of this rucksack, let us consider two kinds of big-game hunting. The *first method*—and the more common—is when you leave your base after a good breakfast, well after daylight, and then hunt and tramp until late afternoon, except for perhaps taking a stand during midday on a good lookout. You wend your way homeward in time to reach camp and supper before dark.

This is the average day's hunt, and it is not productive of much success except by sheer good luck. Big game feeds and travels abroad mostly between the last hour before sunset and the first hour after sunrise. These two extreme hours are worth more than all the rest of the day combined so far as spotting and bagging game is concerned.

If you hunt in the usual way, you are probably spending these two really productive hours either in camp or within a mile or so of there, where game is surely disturbed and alerted if not actually driven out by noises and smells.

With the *second method*, used by the more experienced

still-hunter, you breakfast long before dawn. You leave camp when just enough pale light has smudged across the eastern horizon to enable you to see well enough not to run a branch into an eye or step into a hole. By the time it's light enough to make out your rifle sights, you are well away in undisturbed country. Throughout the daylight hours, you hunt and watch in the bedding or feeding grounds of the game. You turn homeward when the shadows become long and black.

Advantages of an Overnight Bivouac

Or maybe along toward late afternoon, you see ahead a basin or a range that looks like a good game prospect.

Leaving camp well before dawn, Colonel Whelen has journeyed far into undisturbed country, where he still-hunts game in their bedding or feeding grounds.

Perhaps with your glasses you even make out a buck or a bear gorging himself with berries several miles ahead. You elect to make a bivouac where you then are, preferably in some sheltered spot near water, and to resume your hunt the following day in this more promising game country—country that from your base camp you could not reasonably expect to reach and cover, and then return from, in one day.

Such a decision to remain out overnight may also be forced on you when you kill a large animal near sunset, miles from camp, and in the interest of good meat or a fine trophy have to dress and butcher it without delay. This task may occupy you well after darkness has set in, so blackly that you have to build a fire to see to finish the job.

In many such cases, the chances are that you may even have to make a second camp on your final way back to the base and thus to be two nights out. This is real hunting as distinguished from a day's tramp, and of course it pertains more to unspoiled wilderness than to the more populated deer forest adjacent to Eastern farming country.

Hunting in the Canadian Northwest

To be completely factual, there is an exception to this pale dawn to dim dusk hunting. This is in the open country of the Canadian Northwest, where you find sheep, goat, caribou, moose, and bear. These animals here feed and bed largely in the open. They can be seen near noon almost as often as in the wee hours, although if you seek them at watering spots, the early and late portions of the day are still most productive. We often locate game here with binoculars and then stalk them rather than still-hunt.

In such open country, too, you and perhaps your horse

can customarily travel long after the sun goes down. In northern British Columbia, the days become so prolonged that during June, in clear weather, it is possible to read outdoors comfortably at midnight. Hunting in such regions may be considered as a *third method.*

Packing the Rucksack

For the first and third kinds of hunting, you require only some of the articles already mentioned. Unless you are traveling in the saddle or with a pack dog, these items can be most easily and satisfactorily carried in your rucksack. Probably the entire load will be considerably less than ten pounds.

For the second type of hunting, you need to carry food and shelter that will enable you to remain out two nights if necessary. Let us inventory this kind of a hunter's pack.

AMMUNITION

Take the ammunition first. In addition to the cartridges in your rifle, you should have at least two or three rounds in your handiest pocket. These can be wadded in your handkerchief so that they will not rattle. The more convenient and practical way to carry the cartridges is compactly and silently in a clip. This way, making sure of their continued accessibility, you can have them out and headed in the right direction with a single motion.

Then, in your rucksack, carry a full carton of twenty cartridges, five of these being small-game loads. The latter may come in handy for grouse and small mammals you may want to collect either for the pot or, unless prohibited by law, for their pelts. Why so many cartridges? For one reason, you can never tell when some emergency may arise, or when signal shots may be highly desirable.

Your watch, compass, and waterproof matchbox certainly, go along, probably in your pockets unless the compass happens to be one of the convenient pin-on variety. In the rucksack, perhaps, you have a sharp skinning knife and a whetstone with which to keep it that way.

If you expect that you may shoot a moose or other big animal, it will be a good idea also to include one of two things. A small, keen hand-ax weighing not more than a pound is a great aid in butchering large game. So is a light folding saw if you can locate one of sufficiently good quality. If not, a small hacksaw will get through bones a lot more neatly than an ax.

CAMERA AND BINOCULARS

Almost certainly you will want to bring back some record of your hunt, whether it is successful from a trophy standpoint or not. Photographs of animal tracks, new country, and of your bivouac will help you to relive your trip and share it with others for years afterwards. So, you will very possibly wish to include a small camera, an exposure meter, spare film, and a clamp-on holder, which with a self-timer will let you get into the picture. This equipage also goes into the rucksack.

Binoculars, however, should be suspended by the leather thong around your neck so that they will hang in front, just below your collar, where you can bring them to your eyes instantly. There is no need to wear a case. So that the glasses won't bounce around too much or get in the way when I lean forward, I shove mine inside my shirt.

CLOTHING

For clothing, you may need some kind of warm garments for the chill of the morning, or to don while watching on a stand, or to put on at night. A mackinaw or similar coat, if you're walking, is ordinarily too heavy and unwieldy in ratio to the warmth it affords. A down insulated jacket is a better choice in cold weather.

During many years in the wildest and occasionally the coldest portions of the continent, we have found the best extra garment is simply another good woolen shirt. When it becomes too warm, stow it in your rucksack along with a light pair of gloves perhaps, or, during colder weather, woolen mitts (one of the mitts must have a flap-covered slit in the palm through which the trigger finger can be extended).

PONCHO

Another item we would recommend is a poncho. You can secure one weighing only a pound which will fold up as small as a bandanna handkerchief. It will keep even your knees bone-dry in snow and rain. It is protection in a cold wind. It will even serve splendidly for a lean-to shelter when you remain out overnight.

SLEEPING BAG

For sleeping you may like to consider one of the down-filled mummy sleeping bags that weigh only some three or four pounds. These are a little bulky, though, and if you roll one inside your poncho, it will make a bundle about six by fifteen inches which will probably have to be tied on the outside of your rucksack.

GRUBSTAKE

Next we come to grub, briefly because of the detailed chapters on the subject of sustenance toward the end of this book. You are going out from your base camp prepared to spend two nights—seven meals, that is—away from it. You will need sufficient nourishment to keep you warm and stoked with energy. This food should be reasonably free of water and not bulky.

Our own tastes have always been quite simple. We have relied mostly on small waterproof bags containing such

The caribou of the Canadian Northwest feed and bed largely in the open.

staples as rolled oats, cornmeal, whole milk powder, whole egg powder, flour and other ingredients which, when mixed in the correct proportions, provide bannock dough when water is added. We also take along sugar, salt, bacon, figs, dates, raisins, chocolate, tea, and the like. Experiment with these at home, to get an idea of how much it takes to make seven meals that will reasonably satisfy your outdoor appetite. You will probably be surprised at the scant weight and bulk that will suffice.

COOKING AND EATING UTENSILS

For a combination cooking and eating utensil, you will need a small pot with a bail. If you don't want to bother carrying it back, a large fruit-juice can with an attached wire bail will do. You'll also probably want either an enamel or stainless steel cup. An Army aluminum frypan will double as a plate. Any greasy food may be carried inside of this, incidentally.

Add a spoon. You already have your knife. A stick will make a suitable fork, although taking a light stainless steel fork offers no trouble, either. Include, too, a plastic bag about fifteen inches square which will be handy for carrying back any liver, heart, kidneys, and tongue.

So that is the maximum hunter's pack. It will probably weigh somewhere between ten and fifteen pounds. The bulk will be slight. If you carry it in a rucksack low down on your back, you will scarcely notice it all day long.

Siwashing in Comfort

How can you be comfortable siwashing out in the hills and woods on a cold night with so light a rig and without a tent? This is not nearly so difficult as it may seem. When you decide you are going to make a night of it, begin looking for a suitable place to bivouac.

There should be water nearby, of course. Ordinarily, however, it is wise not to bed down close beside it. You will generally find the climate more comfortable a hundred feet or so higher on a beach or hill. There it will be warmer, dryer, possibly quieter, and the air drift will be much less. Try to find a small clump of spruce, balsam, or at least some thick bushes in which your bed will be sheltered from any wind.

For the bed, clean off a level space about three feet wide and a foot longer than your height. Scratch depressions several inches deep for your shoulders and hips. If you want to take the trouble, cut four poles and stake them in place around the edge of this bed. A mattress can be made of shingled evergreen boughs, as described in Chapter 11, or you may simply gather together dry forest litter such as leaves and pines needles. As a matter of fact, the latter will be warmer.

Then haul in a lot of firewood, enough to last all night. This does not have to be short, and you don't need to spend a lot of time working it into any particular lengths. Unless there is a fire hazard, fairly big logs ten to fifteen feet long are fine. You can place the centers in the fire, let the logs burn in two, and then move the ends in easily.

Locate your fire downwind from your bed, lengthwise to it, and about three feet away. Stretch your poncho above the bed as a reflecting tent if you want, and your little camp will be all ready for supper and a night's rest. After you have fueled up on grub, take time to dry out your underwear and socks. Put on the extra shirt. Arrange the rucksack for a pillow if you want.

The best hunting country will be miles away from your base camp; keep close to game by making one-night camps in the hills and woods after the day's hunt.

Build up the fire with the big stuff so that it will hold, and lie down and let your thoughts drift as lazily as the clouds scudding across the yellow moon. In two or three hours, maybe the cold will awaken you. Don't just lie there and shiver; listen to the night noises, the sweetness with which a whippoorwill's call sounds, the wildness of the echoes set vibrating by a dark loon's laugh. Perhaps you'll detect the faint distant cries of migrating swans, of wild wings flapping exultantly nearer, and of tremulous notes that blend vaguely with the music of wilderness water and the melodic muttering of trees.

These small, heartening, one-night camps are among the most memorable you will ever experience, particularly if you are fortunate enough to have a congenial companion along. They will live longer in your thoughts than those nights spent in the base camp with its comparative conveniences. And at the first platinum streak of dawn, you will be rested, fed, and in the best hunting country.

19. Guns and Ammunition for Hunting

For the procurement of such meat as your country affords, you need an adequate rifle. The more efficient this weapon is and the more skilled in its use you have made yourself, the better will be your chance of obtaining pot meat. You should also know where to look for your meat, and the best ways of bringing it to bag. So let us discuss these matters in this chapter.

No piece of equipment I know of has been written about more often than the big-game rifle. The discussion has been endless, much of it among authors who have never shot anything larger than a small deer in a forest close to civilization. There are just two phases of the subject about which I would like to talk with you. The first is the killing power of the cartridge. The second is the refinements of the weapon that will help you to make kills that are sure and humane, preferably with one shot.

Making Sure of Instant Kills

No bullet—no matter how large in diameter, how heavy, or at how high a velocity it is fired—can be depended on to kill big game reliably and swiftly unless it strikes in a vital part of the anatomy. This means the brain, the spinal column, or the center of the animal's blood supply: the heart, the large arteries around it, and the lungs.

The brain and the spinal column present too small targets for anyone to be sure of hitting except under unusual circumstances. The chest, containing the heart and lungs, presents the largest mark. A modern bullet at modern velocity penetrating into this boiler room disrupts so much tissue, and so fills the cavity with blood, that the animal either succumbs on the spot or drops after a wild race of perhaps twenty-five to a hundred yards, as soon as the supply of blood to the brain ceases.

This critical area is not a difficult target. Any hunter who cannot be fairly sure of striking it with the majority of his shots has no moral right to hunt with the rifle, for he will cause too much suffering.

CARTRIDGE WEIGHTS AND CALIBERS

For sure killing, all that is then necessary is a cartridge having a bullet of such weight and construction that, at the velocity at which it is fired, it will smash through the heaviest shoulder blades and ribs surrounding the chest cavity and penetrate within. The minimum bullet that will do this on all species of American big game up to about 200 yards is a soft-point, jacketed bullet of .25 caliber, weighing at least 117 grains, and fired at a muzzle velocity of at least 2,700 feet per second.

As the weight of the bullet goes up, a proportionately lower velocity will still assure the same smash and energy. The minimum is therefore, roughly speaking, the .257 Roberts, or the .300 Savage, or the .35 Remington cartridge.

With heavier cartridges, be sure that the recoil of the weapon does not preclude nail-driving marksmanship on your part. A properly constructed .30-caliber bullet of 180 grains at MV. 2,700 f.s. (.30-06 U.S. cartridge) is adequate for any American big game if properly directed at the chest cavity. But not even it, or anything larger, is sure unless accurately aimed.

Big-Game Rifles

American standard big game rifles are almost invariably equipped with an open rear sight and a bead front sight, both of the vintage of about 1730. Such sights are totally inadequate for the kind of shooting, I trust, the wilderness-loving sportsman will accept. I have coached thousands of men in rifle marksmanship, but I confess I cannot teach anyone to shoot well with a rifle fitted with such obsolete sights.

Of course, you can knock down a deer at fifty yards or a woodchuck at fifty feet, if that is all you require. But in the open and in the woods, the alignment of such sights is so affected by light and shadow as to cause prohibitive errors at longer distances. Moreover, in the hurry and the excitement of shooting at game, scarcely anyone can depend on himself to make the careful alignment necessary with such sights. The common result is overshooting.

Such open sights should always be removed from any rifle you purchase. The rear one should be replaced with a Lyman-type (large peep in a small disc) adjustable receiver sight. We think the best hunting front sight is the Redfield flat-top Sourdough. For the way to aim with these sights, see any of the better manuals on rifle marskmanship.

Such sights can be seen more clearly in poor light than can any other metallic sights. A few days of their use, aimed correctly, will result in much more accurate hitting ability. In the hands of a fair marksman, a lever or pump-action rifle is capable of sure shots on big game up to some 150 yards: the better bolt-action rifles will perform well on out to about 250 yards. So sighted, the old .30-30 Winchester and .250-3000 Savage rifles make fine weapons for deer in wooded country.

The experienced hunter-rifleman of today demands a more specialized rifle that will respond to his skill in marksmanship. At the same time, it must be simple and rugged enough for wilderness use. The past thirty years have seen big strides in the development of such rifles. A bolt-action rifle of better grade is the Winchester Model 70, weighing about 8½ pounds, and chambered for the .20 Winchester or .30-06 U.S. cartridge.

Such a firearm should have a well-fitting and properly bedded stock, a shooting gun sling, and a single-stage trigger pulling off at between three and four pounds pressure without creep or backlash. The rifle is best sighted with a four-power modern hunting telescope sight with a field of view of at least 30 feet at 100 yards. By taking full advantage of the rifles capabilities, an efficient hunter can make sure hits in the boiler room on big game out to about 350 yards. This is the artist's weapon.

SIGHTING

No rifle can be properly sighted at the factory or by a gunsmith except by sheer luck. You must sight it in yourself, both for your way of holding and aiming, and for the ammunition you will use in the woods. Until this has been

The Winchester Model 70, carried by Brad Angier, is a top grade bolt-action rifle, simple and rugged enough for wilderness use.

done, you can place no reliance whatever on your weapon. The task should be taken care of before your trip, and it should be verified several times. Rifles shooting cartridges having a muzzle velocity of 2,500 to 3,000 feet per second should have their sights adjusted to strike the point of aim at 200 yards. They will then not overshoot more than 3 inches at 100 yards. By accurately aiming just a trifle high at 300, or at the top edge of a large animal at 350 yards, you can be sure of a good hit.

Pothunting

The full-charged factory cartridge will blow small edible game and furbearers to smithereens if the bullet strikes in the body. Throughout the wilder parts of the United States and Canada, grouse are not particularly alarmed by human beings. It is common to come on one strutting or dusting on the ground, or to have it fly up onto a lower branch of a tree and offer a standing shot at ten to fifteen yards. You can then decapitate the grouse with your rifle if you know exaclty where the bullet will travel with relation to the point of aim at these short distances. Usually, it strikes an inch to half an inch low.

But the full-charged cartridge releases a lot of noise to echo around a game country, and it is rather like using a sledge hammer to drive a carpet tack. Such cartridges are not particularly good getters of such pot meats. For small game, it is best to use home-loads with low charges of powder that will neither waste meat nor cause too distrubing a report.

The All Around Rifle

Most of you, I imagine, would not care to be burdened with more than one rifle or gun in the woods. In many localities, it is preferable to have a weapon well suited to both large and small game. Such an all-around rifle is the king of weapons for the chronic wilderness lover and loafer. It is based on a .25- to .30-caliber rifle, adapted to use both a light load for small game as well as the standard big-game factory load. This adaptation does not detract one iota from its effectiveness on large animals.

The small load should be adequate for all game from quail and squirrels to turkey and beaver, killing neatly but having no more destructive effect than the .22 Long rifle cartridge. The best light loads are based on the use of the lighter-jacketed bullets with sharp points. Muzzle velocity should not be greater than about 1,600 feet per second. Such a bullet will not expand at this low velocity. Passing through the body of a grouse or weasel, it will neither destroy too much edible meat nor ruin a trophy skin.

For forty years, I have used such a load in my .30-06 rifle with the greatest satisfaction. It consists of the 150-grain, full-jacketed, pointed (M11) service bullet with a powder charge of 18 grains of Du Pont No. 4759 powder. Even better loads are the .25-caliber 87-grain, and the .270-caliber 110-grain, bullets with slightly lighter charges of the same powder.

These loads have slight disadvantages. They give a little louder report than it is desirable to let loose in a terrain where your anticipated trophy is a big-game animal. They require a different adjustment of the sights from that needed for the big-game load, so that you have to shift both cartridge and sights. Finally, these reduced loads cannot be bought on the market. You must handload them yourself or have a custom handloader make them up for you. Handloading ammunition, however, is a most interesting hobby.

For some years now, my favorite all-around rifle and my constant afield has been a bolt-action rifle of nine pounds weight, chambered for the .270 W.C.F. cartridge, and sighted with a four-power Bear Cub scope. For big game, I use either the 150-grain Sierra boat-tail bullet, or the 150-grain Speer sharp-point bullet loaded to M.V. 3,000 f.s.

With the elevation dial of the scope set at two minutes, this load shoots to the point of aim at 200 yards. At 100 yards, it strikes two inches above aim. At 300 yards, it drops about six inches, and it is about a foot low at 350 yards.

The small game load is the 110-grain Sierra pointed, soft-point bullet with a charge of 16 grains of 4759 powder. With the reticule dial of the Bear Cub scope set at seven minutes, the bullet strikes three-tenths of an inch below aim at 25 yards, one inch above aim at 50 yards, and three-fourths of an inch above at 100 yards. At this latter distance, a five shot group will fall within a circle about 1.5 to 1.75 inches in diameter. The report is quite light and the recoil nil.

20. How to Butcher the Game You Kill

A lot of people, particularly women, sincerely believe that they don't care for wild meat. Many such individuals are convinced that they especially dislike deer flesh. They complain that what they describe as venison's gamy taste is too strong. Not a few try to make the meat more edible, to their way of thinking, by horribly overcooking it.

When people react this way to venison, you can bet the animal was not butchered properly at the right time, or that the meat was not cared for as it should have been afterwards.

Sometimes a buck or bull secured at the height of the rutting season is not as good as it might be. A paunch-shot animal that has run a long distance before falling will not make the best venison. Otherwise, given proper and timely butchering and care, all venison when suitably cooked, should be tempting to even the most critical tastes.

Venison, it is true, usually does not taste like our domestic meats. Young bear, however, when properly stewed or roasted, cannot be distinguished by the average individual from choice beef. Mountain sheep always has somewhat the savoriness of lamb, while mountain goat resembles mutton.

Draining the Carcass

When you shoot a large animal, it is ordinarily useless to run in and cut its throat or stick it in the point of the chest with the motive of bleeding it. A modern bullet so disrupts the cavities of the chest or abdomen that they fill with blood almost immediately. Little or none of this blood will come out if the throat is cut.

Besides, you are going to open the animal without delay, anyway. At the very least, if, for instance, you have to follow a second wounded quarry—you will slit open the abdomen and chest and leave the animal, preferably across branches or otherwise in some well-ventilated position, so that it will both drain and cool as soon as possible. In an emergency, all this can be done within a couple of minutes. Under favorable conditions, in cool dry weather when there are no flies, the meat will still be good days later.

In any event, the blood should be drained out just as soon as possible. If you're going to use the skin, don't spill blood on it, for blood is difficult to remove. When the animal has been cleaned out, take fistfuls of grass, moss, or leaves and wipe the chest and abdominal walls free of moisture. Get the inside walls as clean and dry as you can. Never, never use water.

Butchering

When you come to your kill, don't try to hang the animal up unless this can be accomplished easily and quickly. If the job is difficult and unreasonably time-consuming as it ordinarily is, it will be sufficient to have the carcass with the head uphill and the rest of the body slanting downwards. If that is not possible, get the animal's chest up on a rock or log.

Turn the animal belly up, securing it in that position with rocks, logs, stakes, or whatever else may be handy. Then make a three-inch cut at the lower end of the breastbone just below the lowest ribs. As soon as the knife cuts through the skin, fat, and meat into the body cavity, insert the first two fingers of whichever is your master hand into the opening. Hold the intestines down and away so that the knife will not penetrate them. Then extend the incision down to the rectum, circumventing the active external milk glands, if any, and then returning to lift and cut away these easily disengaged tissues. Cut around each side of the major sexual organ and around the rectum, taking care not to puncture either. The contents can quickly taint the best meat unless any areas of accidental contact are immediately trimmed away. Carefully free the ducts leading to the rectum and the sex organ, and tie them off with a piece of string or lace so that nothing will escape from them.

Then with your sleeves rolled up and any wrist watch removed, reach up into the upper end of the abdominal cavity and cut the diaphragm loose all around. This is the membrane that separates the organs of the chest from those in the abdomen. Now reach with your secondary hand into the top part of the chest. Find and pull down on the windpipe, gullet, and large arteries. Cut them off as close to the neck as you can. This is one operation where, because of the close and obscure quarters, you have to take particular care not to slash yourself.

Now the entire contents of the chest and abdomen are free except for occasional adhesions along the backbone. These can be quickly torn free by hand. You can now turn the animal on its side and dump out the viscera. As you work down towards the stern, take care to poke the two tied ends free so that they will fall out with the remainder. After this, wipe the inside of the animal as dry as possible, once you have dragged it away from the discards.

DELICACIES

Save the heart, cutting it free of the little pouch of membrane in which it is lodged. Be sure to lay the liver carefully beside it on some clean area such as a piece of bark, a rock, or a patch of snow. Secure the two kidneys as well. All are delicious. You may also care to save the white sheets of abdominal fat which will make excellent lard for cooking.

Unless you are going to have the head mounted, slit the underneath of the jaw deeply enough so that you can pull the tongue down through this opening and sever it near the base. When we are hunting, we both carry a bloodproof bag in which to stow the heart, liver, kidneys, tongue and fat for carrying back to camp.

Cooling the Carcass

Now turn back to your animal. What you do next will depend to a large extent on circumstances such as weather, weight, and terrain. You may be able to hang your kill up by the head. You will at least be able to turn it so that the body opening can be propped open with sticks so that the meat will cool as soon as possible.

Covering the carcass with a mass of well-leaved boughs will protect the flesh to a large extent from the shifting sun, as well as from birds, such as Canada jays, which may already be waiting for a chance to peck away at the fat.

If blowflies are bad, you should either have enough cheesecloth to cover the cavity or one of those cheesecloth bags available from outfitters in which the entire animal can be placed. Bluebottles and other winged pests will still probably get the carcass to some extent. When these have been particularly thick, we've found it effective to douse the bottom few of a mass of evergreen boughs with a personal fly dope—taking care, of course, to keep this off the meat. In any event, examine all openings and exposed spots when you pack the animal out, and wipe away any eggs and young larvae.

If rain is threatening, a better procedure is to turn the animal so that is is draped back up over a rock or log. The body cavity must be freely ventilated in any exigency. For example, turning a freshly butchered deer on its belly in the snow will cause the meat to start to putrify noticeably overnight, despite temperatures well below zero.

At this point, you will probably leave your kill and go back to camp to secure companions or a pack animal to help in getting the carcass out of the woods. If you are in country where bear are thick, it may be a good idea to discourage their presence by leaving some article of clothing flapping nearby. One of us has had a big blacky and her two cubs clean up the hindquarters of two large bucks we had shot just before sunset and had returned for the next forenoon.

Wolves are far more cautious. We've cleaned out a moose during an early Northern night with a pack howling only yards away in the blackness. Sure they would not bother the meat before we returned, we just left it on the snow. When we went after the animal with a horse the next morning, tracks showed that the seven in the pack never did venture closer than fifty feet.

One other time, however, we had to leave a butchered moose out a week in the mountains because of the weather.

When we got there that time, the snow for a hundred feet all around had been flattened down as slick as a skating rink. Only one shin bone remained within even that area. That was the only instance when timber wolves have ever troubled any of our meat.

Carrying Out the Carcass

The easiest way to get the venison out of the woods is with a horse. This is a common practice in the West. In the East, some hunting camps keep a horse for this purpose. If the animal is spooky, stroke and pet him some and during the process rub a little of the blood on his nose.

Ordinarily, you can tie a deer across or in front of the riding saddle. With something such as a moose, you'll perhaps cut it up and divide the sections between two pack animals. If snow is on the ground, you may drag the unskinned quarry by its head, after cutting off the legs at what is usually thought of as the knees but which are actually the ankles. Dragging is most easily accomplished with a harness.

However, you can take a half-hitch high around the horse's tail, bend back the hair, and then take a second half-hitch around the now doubled tail. The usual saddle horse will then skid even a good-sized moose out without any discomfort if conditions are halfway good. If the experience is a new one, the horse will probably settle down better if you remain in the saddle as much as possible. Snugging the rope around the saddle horn is not such a good idea if you're going more than a few feet.

Deer can be dragged headfirst by a couple of husky hunters. They are often carried on a stout pole, back hanging

down and feet tied up over the timber. The head should also
be lashed up so that it won't dangle and continue to throw
the load off balance. As a matter of fact, a deer lugged more
than a short distance in this fasion will swing so much that
you will very probably soon be weighing the advisability of
cutting a second pole and using the two of them as a
stretcher. This, once the animal has been tied on solidly, can
be carried at any height.

One ordinarily rugged man can carry a deer by himself
unless it dresses out far above 100 pounds. There are two
handy ways of accomplishing this. We prefer to drape the

The carcass of the peccary, one of the finest game animals of the tropics, is carried on a pole, with its back
hanging down and its feet tied up over the timber.

animal over our shoulders like a scarf and to hold onto the legs. This way if you start to slip or stumble, you can get rid of the load in a hurry. If you've tied it into a pack by lashing the legs together, you may fall and find an uncomfortable amount of weight pressing you down. A common way of carrying deer, nevertheless, is by tying all four legs together and then running your head between body and legs, with the shank ends held down in front of your chest with one hand. The flats on the sides of one fore and hind leg then rest on your shoulders and do not cut in. It is almost impossible to carry a heavy deer piggyback for any distance because of the way the sharp bones bite into the shoulders.

If under any circumstances whatsoever you carry a deer through a forest frequented by other hunters, tie a red bandanna handkerchief or strips of bright red cloth conspicuously around it. It isn't a bad idea, either, to sing in a loud voice.

Skinning

Old-time hunters very often prefer to complete the skinning on the spot. You may pretty well have to do this if your trophy is big. There are exceptions, of course depending generally on the available methods of transportation and to some degree on the weather.

In any event, you'll want to get the hide off as soon as reasonably practical. The meat should be allowed to cool thoroughly with the least possible delay. Unless the animal is a small one and is opened wide, it won't cool quickly in temperate weather with the skin on. And if you're in a cold climate, you'll want to complete the skinning before the hide freezes on—or what would have been an hour's work may very easily develop into a cold and disagreeable all-day chore.

For the good of the meat, don't toss a whole deer—skin and all—on the warm front of your car to motor it back that way. It's a very pleasant feeling to drive back to friends and family with the entire animal on display, and in some of the big old cars with high sweeping fenders you could get away with it. In far too many instances, however, the fine delicate flavor of the venison is tainted if not completely spoiled by this practice.

Quartering

Once the carcass is free of the skin, which you have been shifting about so as to keep the meat as clean as possible, quartering will be in order. Unless you intend to save the head, ease the point of your blade deeply into the cartilages between the skull and the first vertebra, severing them as well as you can. Then twist the head abruptly in one direction and then in the other, and it will snap free.

With an ax, or ideally a meat saw, split the bone from the belly cut to the neck. Open the neck longitudinally on the same line and remove the windpipe and gullet. Then split the backbone from neck to tail. The animal will now be in two halves. Quarter it by cutting each of these halves along the line of the lowest ribs.

Protecting the Carcass from Pests

You may now choose to rub flour on these quarters and to wrap them in cheesecloth to discourage pests. Sprinkling black pepper on the flesh will also help to keep bluebottles and such annoyers off. You will also probably want to examine the meat every day or so to make sure that it remains unbothered, giving particular attention to bullet wounds and to folds and nicks in the flesh. Any eggs or larvae so detected can be quickly and harmlessly scraped, wiped, or, if you wish, cut away.

In any event, the quarters can now cool quickly, especially if you hang them high in a tree to hasten the chilling the first night. Some of the pack trains in the Canadian Rockies, hunting early so as to be back down in the lowlands before snow sets in too deeply, keep fresh game sweet by trimming the branches from a tree and pulling the meat up into the clear twenty feet or more from the ground, where blowflies do not operate.

If you have a large enough outfit to warrant its inclusion a meat tent is a handy thing to pack along in hot weather. A handy model, often seen in survey camps in the wilderness, consists of canopied netting with a zipper opening. This shelter is customarily tied in a dark, well-ventilated spot by a single rope that runs from its top center.

Refrigeration

Keep these quarters as cool and as dry as possible. If you are heading out of the wilderness, get them into refrigeration as soon as you can. If a long and warm auto trip lies ahead, try at the earliest opportunity (1) to pack each quarter in a carton of dry ice and (2) to secure those containers in larger ones with crumbled newspapers between for insulation. Circumstances may be such, too, that you'll prefer to travel in the comparative coolness of the night.

If the weather is hot and the distance far, you will

probably do well to lay over a day in some locality where you can have the meat frozen solid. This may be a desirable time to cut and wrap it in plainly labeled packages that can be retrieved from the freezer and used one by one. Odd portions can be ground into hamburger, along with a desirable proportion of beef fat.

It should then be an easy job, with the help of dry ice, to bring these packages frozen to your cold storage cabinet, drawer, locker, or butcher's cold room. You'll have some really fine meat.

21. Tasty Ways to Prepare Meat

There is a saying that all meat is grass. This is literally true. The carnivores live on the herbivores. Man lives on both and on grass, in the form of vegetation, as well.

Since meat is grass, it is entirely possible for man to live on meat alone. This has been demonstrated in innumerable instances over the ages, the only requisites being that the meat is largely fresh, that it is not overcooked, and that it is sufficiently fat—the best guide for the latter requirement being the diner's own appetite. When in the normal, unhurried course of a meal you have eaten enough fat, you will want no more.

No particular parts of the animal or fish need to be eaten. Sizzling plump sirloins, if that is what you prefer, will supply you with all the food ingredients necessary for good health even if you eat nothing else whatsoever for a week, a month, or a year.

Vilhjalmur Stefansson, the eminent Arctic explorer, lived in the North for an aggregate of more that five years on meat and water alone. In fact, skins also provided much of his parties' clothing. Under medical supervision centered in New York City, Stef later showed the complete sufficiency of such an all-meat diet by living for a minutely observed and painstakingly tested year exclusively on meat.

You fellows, young and old, who go into the woods and mountains for your vacations, or on rivers and lakes, can get along very nicely for a week or two on imperishable meats such as bacon, ham, dried beef, and the endless canned varieties. But the day soon comes when you crave real, fresh meat to supplement your other foods.

Both Brad and I have left camp a lot of mornings with no provisions for lunch but a blackened pail and a little bundle of tea, figuring to dine—and almost never failing to do so— on some prevalent small game as ptarmigan or partridge. The game we would spit on a stick, thrust briefly into flame both to seal in the juices and to set the flavor, and then roast as slowly as our patiences would allow.

All is meat that comes to a hungry man's table, and all animals and birds in North America are edible. The only exceptions may be polar bears and some seals, which become so excessively rich in Vitamin A that they are poisonous to some degree at certain times—to dogs, incidentally, as well as humans—and are usually as well avoided.

Some animals taste better to each of us than do others. Perhaps none surpass the ungulates or hoofed animals. Of these, mountain sheep is usually considered the most choice, and then caribou, deer, antelope, moose, and goat. Such large animals will provide a lot of nourishment for a long time for many people, and it would be nothing less than a crime to kill any for food unless all the meat is really needed and can be utilized.

Individual amimals and birds of the same species are not equally fine eating in the sense of being tasty and tender. Male animals shot during the rutting season, as a rule, are not so good. The most magnificent trophy that adorns the walls of my hearth room is that of a mountain caribou that I shot one September during the height of the rut. Its meat was something else again. Paunch-shot animals that have run some distance before falling and animals that have been poorly butchered are not such pumpkins. The proper preparation and care of wild meat for food is discussed in the preceding chapter.

Coons, possums, rabbits, and squirrels are all good. In the tropics there are many small exotic animals, among which I would give first place to the sloth despite its unattractive appearance. It is a pure vegetarian, and a far cleaner animal than any pig. Its meat is like delicious pork.

Then there is the whole feathered tribe, all good eating and most of them delicious, although I personally would draw the line at the turkey buzzard. I did try an Amazon parrot once, but I think it had been feeding on a rubber tree; at least, my teeth sort of bounced off. The wild turkey is the most preferred of all wild birds, but you must remove its craw as soon as you have shot it or you are in for a disappointment. As a matter of fact, all birds should be drawn as soon as they are bagged.

The one dish that has lingered longest in my memory was comprised of six-inch brook trout and many frogs' legs which two of us twelve year-old kids prepared alongside a brook in the North Woods. The iguana, that five-and-a-half-foot lizard that looks like the dragon of mythology and which is plentiful in our tropics, is almost the equal of the northern bullfrog. The meat of all the water turtles, except for the livers makes delicious stews.

Then, of course, there are fish, but I shall not touch on such obvious food here except to say that, even if you are not a confirmed angler, it will pay to include some simple light tackle even in a backpacking outfit in case you pass promising waters in your wanderings.

Don't be squeamish in your eating, or you will pass up a lot of really delicious pot meat. Most prejudices have their foundation in ignorance. Stefansson once said that on his expeditions, he much preferred "well-brought-up young

The meat of the Dall sheep is particularly delectable.

men" to more sturdy backwoodsmen, mainly because the former looked on an expedition as a sporting venture and were willing to try anything, while the backwoodsman rebelled at anything that he had not been accustomed to all his life.

The fact is that every animal in the far and near places of this continent, all the fish that swim in our lakes and rivers and streams, and each bird that inhabits the air is good to eat. and newts is edible, furthermore, even to the somewhat bland antlers that are not half bad roasted when they are in velvet, and to the bitterish gall that has an occasional use as seasoning.

Bear

Our carnivores—the meat-eating bears, cats, wolves, and such—are all edible, some individuals more so than others. Summer-killed grizzlies that have been subsisting along salmon streams would not appeal to many, but a young grizzly I shot at timber line one fall was consumed in its entirety, with great gusto, by my companion and myself.

As for black bear, those of us who dine on it regularly, whenever we can, are just about unanimous in the opinion that the mountains and woods afford no more palatable and delicious game meat with the single exception of mountain sheep. Not even cubs and yearlings furnish really good steaks, it is true. But cub, yearling, or oldster all cook up into moist and savory roasts and stews. The meat then so resembles prime beef that you can serve it as such to individuals who are rabidly if unreasonably prejudiced against bear, actually have them coming back for third and forth helpings.

BEAR FAT AS SHORTENING

Any excess fat—and ordinarily there will be considerable, except during the latter stage of hibernation and within the first few lean weeks following—should be trimmed off before the bear meat is cooked. This fat should then be heated in open pans to extract the grease. Strained into tins, the fat of the black bear hardens into a clear white solid that is the best shortening you will ever find.

It is not unusual to get some forty pounds of such lard from a large black bear downed just before the long winter sleep. The shortening procured from a grizzly is also excellent but, when similarly rendered, remains an oil which is not so easily carried. Some backwoodsmen still make spreads for their bannock and flapjacks by mixing some sweet, such as honey or molasses, with bear grease.

BEAR KIDNEYS

Bear kidneys, when the fine membrane about them has been removed, come apart in small individual segments. Stewing these with butter, salt, pepper, celery, dried parsley, chopped onions, a dash of cloves if you happen to have any, and a bit of flour for thickening makes one the choicest wilderness delicacies available.

Some recipes recommend soaking kidneys, liver, heart, tongue, and other such tidbits in cold and sometimes salted water for an hour or so before cooking. Actually, although you can suit yourself, there is no good reason for this, and it takes away a certain amount of flavor and nutriment.

Preserving Meat Juices in Cooking

Most wild meat, unlike bear, is apt to be rather dry. For

venison as venison *should* be, therefore, make sure that the steaks, chops, and roasts are not overcooked. A good general rule is to cook deer, moose, caribou, elk, and similar meat at one-fourth less time than you would lamb.

The tougher portions, such as the neck and the lower hams, can be reserved for stews. The neck, incidentally, also makes the most praiseworthy mincemeat. The ribs are best broiled very quickly over a charcoal or wood fire so you almost burn the exterior but leave the inside nearly raw.

To keep your meat juicy and appetizing, always try, except in the case of soups, to sear the outside quickly in flame, or extreme dry heat, or very hot fat, or furiously boiling water. Then only minimum amounts of the juices will escape. For the same reason, do not use salt until the very end.

Cooking on a Stick

This is the easiest, quickest, and often the handiest way to cook tender meat, and there are no dishes to wash afterward. Take a peeled stick, perhaps a half-inch in diameter and some three feet long, and sharpen both ends. Impale on it chunks of succulent meat about the size of baseballs. Best for this purpose are the long outside strips cut from either side of the backbone; next best, the pair of tenderer but less flavorful tenderloins that lie along the inside of the spine. Between each segment, stick a thick piece of fat or bacon to baste the lean meat.

You can have your fire burning up with a high blaze if you want. Plant the stick upright, close enough to the flames so that the outside of the meat will be quickly seared. Rotate the holder frequently, leaning it at different angles so that the tidbits will cook evenly and rapidly until they are a little

One large black bear can provide some forty pounds of
lard—the best shortening you'll ever find.

bit charred on the outside but still rare and juicy in the
middle. Eat from the stick, salting to taste if you want.

Steaks

Steaks may also be cooked without untensils by extending the meat over glowing embers on forked green sticks.
One of the campfire grates available from most outfitters is
handy for such broiling, too.

Cut the steaks an inch and a half thick if that's the way
you like them, sear them first in flame, and then allow them

to broil three or four minutes to a side some three inches above the live coals of some hardwood such as oak, birch, or maple. The softwoods make poor coals, so it is just as well not to try to broil with them if some better fuel is available. Steaks can also be well broiled atop a dry metal sheet or in a dry frypan.

A lot of campers like to fill a frypan with plenty of sizzling hot lard or bacon grease. They then drop steaks about half an inch thick into the pan one at a time, gradually so that the fat does not stop sputtering. Then steaks are removed, to a hot dish, seasoned, and served.

Boiled Meat

Cut meat for boiling into about two-inch cubes. Drop these one by one into rapidly bubbling water. Don't salt until almost ready to serve. Meat can be relished after it has been boiling only five minutes, but many prefer to let it simmer for an hour or more.

Often rice and other vegetables are cooked along with the meat, and these dictate to some extent the amount of cooking. In any event, the addition of such components should be so staggered that everything will be done at the same time. Any additional fluid that needs to be put in should be boiling, not cold. It is best to keep the pot well covered.

Stews

Stew meat, which can be the toughest in the critter, is best browned in the bottom of the kettle at the outset with grease, chopped onion, and any desired spices. You can then, if you want, stir in enough flour to make a thick smooth gravy.

The liquid comes next. You can use at various times any fluid in which vegetables have been cooked or canned, broth from boiled meat, or just plain aqua pura. Season, bring to a boil, and then cover tightly so it will simmer all morning or all afternoon.

A Dutch oven is a handy receptacle for stew inasmuch as you can dig a hole—always in a safe place where fire cannot spread—and leave it buried there among hot coals while you spend the day hunting.

The preceding is the basis of a stew, and from that point forward you're on your own. What the end result will be depends more or less on ingenuity, imagination, and the materials at hand. Available vegetables go well in such a stew. So do odds and ends of steaks and roasts.

A lot of us, when we are off by ourselves, tend to go in for one-dish meals. This we can easily accomplish with numerous such mulligans, even to the extent of making bread unnecessary by adding a starch such as rice, potatoes, noodles, macaroni, one of the cooked cereals, or perhaps a steaming soft dome of dumplings.

Soup

If you are making soup with a meat base, put the meat in cold salted water. Include any bones you may have, opening the larger of these to get to the marrow, which in terms of energy is the most nutritious part of any animal. Using a saw will do away with sharp splinters. Bring to a boil and let simmer, the longer the better.

Bacon

The main troubles that camp cooks experience with bacon arise from their submitting it to a lot too much heat. Not only is the bacon thus burned and toughened, but very often the frypan becomes a mass of leaping flames. Aside from resulting offenses to taste and digestion, this is wasteful if nothing worse. The nearly 3,000 calories per pound that fat side bacon contains lie largely in its grease, any excess of which should be saved, particularly in the bush.

We'll do better to fry the bacon slowly over a few coals drawn to one side of the blaze. More satisfactory still is the practice of laying the strips well apart in a pan and baking these evenly to a golden brown in a moderately warm reflector baker.

Slabs of bacon have a tendency to mold. Mold can be harmlessly wiped off with a clean cloth moistened either in vinegar or in a solution of baking soda and water.

Lard

The lard pail can be replenished by pouring in your surplus bacon grease. Excellent lard can also be secured from game fat not eaten along with the lean. Cut this into small cubes and, if only in sparse amounts, melt these down in the frypan over a very slow fire.

Pour the liquid grease into some handy container, where ordinarily it will harden and become easy to pack anywhere. Half-pound pipe tobacco cans with pressed top lids are fine for this and other food-packing purposes. Save the cracklings to eat with lean meat or for lunch some cool noon.

Lynx

Lynx meat, served up to hearty appetites alongside a campfire, is, except for fiber, indistinguishable from the white meat of chicken. Because the larger lynx in particular is apt to be somewhat stringy, we like to cut the meat into very small pieces and to fricassee these.

This you can do in a Dutch oven if you want, preparing the meal before you leave camp in the morning and leaving it to reach a state of perfection by the time you return ravenous at night. Or if someone is going to be in camp during the morning or afternoon, the meat can be trusted to cook slowly in a big kettle suspended over the fringes of the fire.

Start the meat as you would a stew in the bottom of a large receptacle. Allow to simmer gently until tender. Such vegetables as onions, carrots, chopped celery, and in fact any you'd include with chicken go equally well with this dish.

You can make gravy on the side if you want by blending six tablespoons of flour with a small amount of cold water, then adding three cups of the liquor from the pot and stirring until a thick sauce is the result. This may be poured over the lynx and vegetables. The fricassee goes well atop mashed potatoes, steaming bannock, or fluffy rice. A little paprika will give it character. The flavor is surprisingly delicate.

Beaver

Among the small animals, the cream of the gourmet crop is our beaver, from the tip of its nose to the end of its tail, although few of us today will have an opportunity to indulge in this delicacy. I still lick my chops thinking of the meals I made from *amisk*, as the Crees call them, on three separate occasions.

One way to collect a luxuriant grizzly robe in the continental Northwest is to accompany a trapper when he goes out in the spring for beaver. The great bears are so fond of fresh beaver meat that it is not unusual for them to raid a camp while the trapper is elsewhere on his line. Once you've sat down to a feed of *amisk* after a day of making your way past steaming snowdrifts and flooded streams, you'll appreciate why.

Beaver meat is particularly rich. When possible, it's best to stick to the tender youngsters. If you ever do cook up one of the big fellows weighing forty or fifty pounds, a good thing to remember is that the meat will become more and more fibrous and stringy the longer it is cooked.

The ordinarily moist dark flesh is reminiscent of plump turkey. It is particularly excellent roasted, and when so cooked it has the advantage of not requiring any basting. Cold, it is still moist and tasty in sandwiches.

Beaver tails are the *piece de resistance* that impelled Horace Kephart to note regretfully when the twentieth century was newer, "This tidbit of old-time trappers will be tasted by few of our generation, more's the pity!"

The first such tails that Brad ever saw in a detached state were presented to him by a Northern trapper, Dan Macdonald, who'd strung a dozen on a cord. In this form, they look like nothing quite so much as scaly black fish whose heads have been removed. Heat caused the rough dark skin to puff and lift away, exposing a white and gelatinous meat. Somewhat resembling pork when boiled, this goes particularly well with such dishes as baked beans and thick pea soup.

Properly seasoned, and dried for about a month, game will keep indefinitely.

Preserved Meat

If you're camping in one place and have a quantity of fresh meat you'd like to preserve with a minimum of trouble, cut it into strips about the size of the average forearm, following the membranous divisions among the muscles as much as possible. Pull off as much of this parchment as you can.

Roll the pieces in a mixture made in the proportions of three pounds of table salt, five tablespoons of black pepper, and four tablespoons of allspice. You can then either drape the strips over a wire or similar support where they'll be safe from animals small and large, or you can pierce one end and hang each with a piece of string.

The meat must be kept dry. About a month is needed for it to shrink and season properly. After that, it will keep indefinitely. Moose we've preserved in this way has lasted a dozen years, by which time the last chunk has been eaten. This tastes good when thinly sliced and chewed on the trail. Scraped and trimmed some, it goes well in mulligans.

JERKY

Jerky is very concentrated and nourishing. A little goes a long way in rations light in weight and high in nourishment. This pioneer stand-by is not by itself a good food for long-continued consumption, however, as it lacks the necessary fat.

The fat, which would turn rancid, should be trimmed away from the meat before the drying operation necessary for jerky is commenced. A conservative procedure is to render it, either for later use as a food supplement or for more immediate employment in the making of pemmican.

Jerky is lean meat that has been divided into strips and dried over a fire or in the sun. Its manufacture is commenced by cutting lean beef, venison, or other fresh red meat into long, wide strips about half an inch thick. Hang these on a wood framework about four to six feet off the ground.

Under this rack, build a small, slow, and smoky fire of any nonresinous wood. This fire should not be hot enough to cook the meat at all, its chief use being to keep flies away. Let the meat dry in the sun and wind. Cover it at night and if rain falls. It should dry in several days.

When jerked, the meat will be hard, and it will be more or less black outside. Protected from dampness and from insects, it will keep almost indefinitely. It is best eaten just as it is. Bite off a chunk and chew. Devoured thus, it is quite tasty, especially when ambling along a wilderness trail gives you the time and the relaxed perspective necessary for fully savoring it. Jerky may also be cooked in stews and soups.

PEMMICAN

Pemmican is little known and eaten these days. Any manufactured products labeled "pemmican" that we have sampled have been a long cry from real pemmican. Without doubt, however, this is one of the most perfect foods there is, especially for use during long journeys in the remote regions.

Indians in British Columbia smoke-drying game into jerky.

To make pemmican you start with jerky. Pound this into small shreds, perhaps with the back of your ax. Then take a lot of raw animal fat. Good beef fat, for example, can be purchased from your butcher at very slight cost. Cut the fat into small pieces about the size of walnuts. Try these out in the frypan over moderate heat, never letting the grease boil up.

When the grease is all out of the lumps, discard these or give them to your dog. Pour the hot grease over the shredded jerky, mixing the two together until you have about the consistency of ordinary sausage. Then pack the pemmican in waterproof bags. The Indians used skin bags. No salt at all should be added.

Ideal pemmican is, by weight, approximately one-half rendered fat and one-half well-dried lean meat. Approximately five pounds of fresh lean meat is required to make one pound of jerky suitable for pemmican.

True pemmican of this sort comes close to being the one perfect food for any length of time, as it contains all the elements for perfect nourishment with the single exception of Vitamin C which, if you are already in good health, you can do without for close to two months. However, supplementing the pemmican with fresh fish, fresh rare meat, or any other fresh and not overcooked food such as the rose hips you can often pick while walking along, will supply the Vitamin C needed to prevent scurvy.

22. Groceries for Camping Trips

Such names as jerky, buccan, parched corn, pemmican, and pinole remind us that dehydrated foods were important on this continent back during pioneer days. The formula has not changed. It is to remove as much water from the edible part of the particular food as may be practicable. Drying by wind and sun often extracted no more than three-quarters of this moisture. Present processes sometimes leave less than a fraction of 1 percent.

Pinole is a flour ground from parched corn. It was used by our primitive Indians and early frontiersmen as an emergency food. As such, it is still valuable, although these days you may have to make your own. This is not too difficult if you or a friend have an electrically equipped kitchen for grinding. Backpackers who have to strip down to a minimum weight and bulk may find it useful to include some pinole in their outfits.

Two tablespoons of pinole stirred into a cup of cold water make a rather insipid and tasteless gruel which, nevertheless, sticks to the ribs at times when you need energy. To make it more appetizing, you can add a spoonful of milk powder and another of powdered chocolate to the mixture, at the same time doubling the amount of water.

Here are a few of the available items that you may want to consider for your next grub list.

POWDERED MILK

Dried skim milk has all the nourishment of fresh skim milk. It contains all the elements that make liquid skim milk such an important food—calcium, phosphorous, iron, and other minerals, B vitamins, natural sugar, and protein. Powdered whole milk has all these, plus the fat and Vitamin A found in the cream of whole milk. Adding two teaspoons of butter or margarine to a cup of reconstituted skim milk, will make it equal in food value to a cup of whole milk.

Containers of dried milk should be kept tightly closed, as the powder attracts moisture and becomes lumpy if long exposed to air. It also picks up odors unless care is taken, as some of our trapper friends using pack dogs have found out.

Milk powder is sometimes a little difficult to mix with water, but there are several ways to get around this. When you open the container, stir the powder and take up the amount you want lightly and without packing it down in any way. Even measures are best obtained by leveling off the top of the cup or spoon with the straight edge of a knife. Place the powder on top of the water with which it is to mix. Then stir with a spoon until smooth. The mixing can be speeded somewhat by having the water slightly warm. You can also shake the water and powder together in a tightly closed jar which will then serve as a pitcher. Dehydrated milk that dissolves almost instantly is now on the market.

Powdered milk, mixed dry with the flour, makes a valuable addition to biscuits and other breadstuffs. When you're in a hurry to get away hunting or fishing, milk powder can be mixed directly with cereals such as oatmeal, and the breakfast food can then be cooked as indicated on the package.

POWDERED EGGS

An egg is 11 percent waste unless you bake the shells and then pulverize them, as a lot of bushmen do for increasing the calcium content of their dogs' food. Of the remaining yolk and white, 74 percent is water. Yet a dried whole egg has practically the same food values, includes no waste whatsoever, and is only 5 percent water.

Varying somewhat with different brands, one pound of dried eggs is the equivalent of three dozen or more fresh eggs. Two level tablespoons of the powder mixed with two and a half tablespoons of water usually equals one hen's egg. Used in such dishes as cakes and puddings, desiccated whole eggs cannot be detected from eggs you have to crack open.

Cooked by itself, the flavor of egg powder is different from that of fresh eggs. Most of us on this continent are accustomed to the latter, so our natural reaction is that the former is inferior. But with a different premise, it works the other way, too. In any event, powdered eggs scrambled with bacon, chopped liver, kidneys, or dried meat make appetizing dishes.

Scrambled eggs made from the powder come to taste mighty good in the bush. Dissolve egg powder and dehydrated milk in lukewarm water to make the proportions of fresh eggs and milk you ordinarily use. Add salt, pepper, and a chunk of butter or margarine. A little flour may be used for thickening. Scrambling all this with bacon gives the dish added flavor.

POWDERED BEVERAGES

For camp use, powdered instant coffee is far preferable to the ground article. It is more economical in weight and bulk, cheaper, better-lasting, and both quicker and easier to prepare. It can be made to individual order and without waste. Furthermore, there is no coffee pot with its darned spout to clean afterwards.

There is considerable difference in flavors, and you should ascertain your favorite before outfitting. Habit will do the rest. Powdered cream may be carried along, too, if you want.

If you'd like to provide for a quick pickup that you can take without the bother of stopping, as when you're hot on the trail of a moose, mix a teaspoon of your favorite powdered coffee with two teaspoons of sugar. Two or three of these combinations can each be wrapped in a bit of foil and stowed in a pocket. One, plopped dry into the mouth, will afford the same stimulation as would a cup of coffee.

Tea was something we long preferred to carry in the usual form, if only for the pleasant rite of tossing a handful of palm-measured leaves into the bubbling kettle. Besides, some of the early concentrates we tried were pretty sad. Now, however, there are powdered teas on the market that mix immediately with warm water and which taste a lot closer to regular tea than any of the powdered coffees taste like regularly brewed coffee. This tea can hardly be spoiled by improper making, although I suppose some camp cook, by trying to make enough for everyone at once, can somehow manage to boil it.

Fruit juices are particular treats in the bush. Lemon, for example, is sometimes welcome with fresh rainbow trout and with salmon. A number of concentrated fruit juices are now available, both dried and liquid.

Bouillon cubes and powders make hot drinks that taste good around a campfire. A lot of times you'll appreciate them a lot more than you would either tea or coffee. They are also useful for flavoring broths, soups, gravies, and stews. Other worthwhile beverage concentrates include cocoa, malted milk, and chocolate.

THE BEAN FAMILY

The various dry beans and their cousins, the dry peas and lentils, are favorite old-time dehydrated foods. All provide hearty nourishment because of their carbohydrates, which the human body transforms into energy. They contain some B vitamins. Besides such minerals as iron and calcium, they furnish protein which the body needs for building and repairing its organs and tissues. They are, furthermore, both inexpensive and fairly easy to prepare.

Although split peas and lentils may be cooked without soaking, beans and whole peas should be soaked, preferably overnight. However, they can be started by first bringing the water to a boil for two minutes. After they have then been soaked for one hour, they will be ready to cook. The brief cooking, too, will guard against any souring if they are to be soaked overnight in warm weather. Cooking should be done in the same water as the soaking, so as to preserve flavor and to conserve vitamins and minerals.

For camp use, canned baked beans leave me sort of cold. It is true they can be prepared "in just a minute or so," but look at the bulk and weight of the cans. I much prefer the old-fashioned dried variety with salt pork. Although it takes hours of preparation, I like to eat a big mess of genuine baked beans every three or four days in camp. They stick to

COOKING DRY BEANS, PEAS, AND LENTILS

	Start with 1 cup of	*Soak in water*	*Add 1 teaspoon salt and boil gently*	*Will yield at least*
Black beans	3 cups	About 2 hours	2 cups
Blackeye beans	2½ cups	1/2 hour	2½ cups
Cranberry beans	3 cups	About 2 hours	2 cups
Great Northern beans	2½ cups	1 to 1½ hours	2½ cups
Kidney beans	3 cups	About 2 hours	2¼ cups
Lentils	2¼ cups	1/2 hour	2¼ cups
	(no soaking needed)		
Lima beans, large	2½ cups	1 hour	2½ cups
Lima beans, small	2½ cups	About 45 minutes	2 cups
Navy (pea) beans	3 cups	About 2½ hours	2½ cups
Peas, split.	*Best made into soup as they break up easily during cooking*		
Peas, whole	2½ cups	1 hour	2½ cups
Pinto beans	3 cups	About 2 hours	2½ cups

the ribs. And the cooking is a good occupation for a rainy day when you have to keep the campfire going anyway.

But if you are bean-hungry and don't want to waste that much time hanging around camp, you can heat up a meal of seasoned precooked beans in less than ten minutes.

Like the old German Erbswurst, pea and bean powders now available make excellent and filling soups in a few minutes. Stir these concentrates in hot water and bring everything to a boil, making the soup as thick as you like it.

OTHER DEHYDRATED FOODS

Dried apples, pears, peaches, apricots, and prunes have long been camp favorites. So have raisins, currants, dates, and figs.

Numerous soup powders are available, and so is an equally large variety of puddings and gelatin desserts. There is even a dehydrated applesauce.

A french-toast mix is for sale. So is a pizza mix. Other combinations offer the camper bran muffins, various regular breads, gingerbread, biscuits, flapjacks of one type and another, waffles, and cakes. There are packaged frostings that need only to be mixed and spread on.

Spaghetti, macaroni, noodles, and the like are already pretty well dehydrated, but now one can purchase different powdered sauce mixes with which to season and flavor them. Hashes are available, of course. Both instant and quick-cooking rices will, if you want, save your time. There is a powder that, dissolved in hot water, makes maple syrup satisfying enough even to these two campers who've spent a good many months in northern New England.

DRY FOODS YOU CAN PACKAGE YOURSELF

Such items, such as bannock—elementarily a cup of flour, ¼ teaspoon salt, and 1 teaspoon baking powder—you may care to package yourself at home. The portions could be just large enough, for example, for a lunch beside the trail. When you are ready to eat, all you need is water.

A dry chocolate pudding mix can be blended at home by mixing and sifting three times: ¾ cup sifted flour, 4 cups skim or whole milk powder, 2 teaspoons salt, 2 cups of sugar, and 2 cups of cocoa. To use, add to each cup of mix 1½ cups of water. Cook over boiling water fifteen minutes, stirring. After the pudding is cooked, add a tablespoon of edible fat and a half-teaspoon of vanilla flavoring, if you want.

Excellent for packaging all such home mixes are the small plastic bags, available very inexpensively from outfitters, which can be readily sealed by a hot iron. If you want to use them again, however, you can close them with Scotch tape.

Sourdough Bread

When a certain musical-show dancer and producer married one of these two writers and went to live in the wilderness of northern British Columbia, the most trouble she had with cooking was in learning how to make flour, salt, sugar, water, and leavening come out bread. But let Vena Angier tell it for herself:

"Sourdough bread was what I wanted, a seventy-year-old trapper, our nearest neighbor, eventually told me. Old-timers in the gold lands of the north are still called sourdoughs, the name borrowed directly from that mining-camp bread that early proved its ability to rise in any temperature short of freezing. On very cold nights, though, this particular sourdough admitted seriously, he still takes the batter to bed with him.

"During the gold-rush days at the turn of the century, when gravel punchers stampeded past our Peace River homesite toward where nuggets lay yellow and beckoning beneath the aurora polaris, prospectors used to bake sourdough bread in the shallow steel vessels they used for panning gold. Some of them still do, for that matter.

"A shallow hole was scooped in the ground, often in the heat-retaining sand of a stream bank. A fire was allowed to burn to coals in this cavity. Dough, in the meantime, was rising between two gold pans. Some of the glowing embers and hot sand were shoveled out of the hole. The pans were sunk in the depression and covered with the hot residue. One hour's cooking, in this makeshift Dutch oven, was generally the minimum. The bread wouldn't burn if allowed to remain longer. The crust would just thicken and become more golden.

"A simple bush method for starting the sourings which are necessary for this breadstuff, our friend Dudley Shaw said, is to mix four cups of flour with enough warm water to make a thick creamy batter. Two tablespoons of sugar may be added. So may two teaspoons of salt. The mixture should be placed in a warm spot for upwards of two days to sour.

"'Cover the sourings loosely,' Dudley cautioned cheerily, 'or they'll explode frightfully all over the place. Makes a ghastly mess. Remember they bubble copiously to better than double size, so use a container that's vast enough.'

"'The initial loaves are made,' Dudley went on, 'by mixing three-fourths of this sourdough with a tablespoon of melted fat and a cup of flour in which a teaspoon of baking soda has been well stirred. Then add whatever additional flour may be necessary to make a smoothly kneading dough.

"'Keep attacking,' the trapper cautioned, eyes blinking amiably behind thick-lensed spectacles. 'Don't gentle it. That is where most women make their mistake. Too much pushing and pressing lets the gas escape that's needed to raise the stuff. Just bank the dough together in a hurry, cut off loaves to fit your pans, and put them in a warm place to rise.'

"The batch, once it has plumped out to double size, should be baked from forty minutes to one hour in a warm oven of one sort or another that is, preferably hottest the first fifteen minutes. Baking should redouble the size of the loaves. One tested 'in the usual way,' Dudley said. He elucidated that the usual job is to wait until the loaves seem crisply brown, then to jab in a straw. If the bread is done, the straw comes out dry and at least as clean as it was when inserted.

"'How about the quarter of the sourdough I don't use?' I inquired, scribbling down the formula.

"That would be my start for further sourdough if it weren't for something else, the trapper told me. These sourings I could keep going by dropping in chunks of left-over bread, flippers, and such, or just plain flour and water. About a cup should always be left out to keep going with.

"When the mixture got too rampageous, a touch of baking soda would gentle it. I should not use soda too copiously, though, or I'd bog down the noble sourdough for good. As a matter of fact, if too much soda is used, it makes the breadstuff yellowish. But it you don't get in enough, then the food tastes sour. A certain amount of experience is required, in other words.

"'That would be your start for future sourdough,'" Dudley Shaw said in a friendly way, 'if it weren't for the fact going to give you some sourings that are fourteen years old.'

"'Fourteen years?' I gasped. 'Isn't that a lot?'

"'They've just started nicely,' Dudley beamed proudly."

This starter in dry form, ready to be activated by water, is now sold for a dollar, plus 50 cents postage and handling, as the Bradford Angier Sourdough Starter by Chuck Wagon Foods, Micro Drive, Woburn, Massachusetts 01501. Once you have it, you will essentially be growing your own yeast; so one packet will last a lifetime.

23. Water for Drinking and Washing

Water from springs and streams that flow from clean and uninhabited North America country can usually be considered safe for drinking and cooking. In the wilderness lake regions of the northern United States and Canada, the water from these bodies is also usually pure—unless there are many camps on the shores or along the courses running into them. This does not always hold true, however. Even if it did, we are not always familiar enough with a region to know what the condition of a watershed may be a short distance away.

Whenever you have the slightest doubt about whether or not water is pure, it should be treated as though unsafe. This includes not only the water you drink. It also involves the water you use for cooking and for washing both cooking utensils and your face.

Cooking and eating implements that have been washed in contaminated water can carry disease germs even though the cooking water is pure or is boiled in the process of cooking. In some localities, uncooked vegetables such as lettuce and radishes are unsafe. Water can often be cleared by letting it seep into a hole dug a few feet from a shore, but such filtration does not insure purity.

Purifying Water

The easiest and most practical way to sterilize doubtful water is to boil it. At or near sea level, hard boiling for five minutes will do the job. For every additional 1,000 feet in altitude, increase the boiling time one minute. (Or add 8 drops of fresh tincture of iodine to even cold water and let stand 30 minutes.)

METHODS THAT DON'T WORK

We've all seen individuals drinking water from dubious sources with the idea that the liquor they were adding to it rendered it safe. This is not the case. The addition of alcohol to water does not rid the water of germs.

Freezing doesn't sterilize water, either. Ice is no more pure than was the water from which it was frozen. Although heat destroys bacteria and parasites, cold very definitely does not.

How to Cool Water in a Hot Climate

In warm country, water may be chilled without ice to a temperature that makes it fairly palatable by the use of water-cooling bags. These hold up to several gallons and are slightly porous, so that a little fluid continues to seep out and to wet the outside. This exterior moisture evaporates in the air and so lowers the interior temperature.

The process may be quickened by hanging the bag in a breeze. This water you can purify at the same time by dropping in the necessary iodine.

Water from Snow

The only precaution that need be taken with pure snow in the wilderness is to treat it like ice cream and not put down too much at once when overheated or chilled. Aside from that, clean snow can be safely eaten any time we are thirsty in the bush.

Wilderness snows, after all, afford in flake form the purest of distilled water obtainable from the atmosphere. Snow's primary drawback is that, proportionately, a considerable amount is required to equal the desired quantity of water. You soon learn to break off sections of any available crust. Heavy granular snow from former storms, is usually more convenient still.

This low water content is quickly evident the first time you melt snow in the noon tea pail. Paricular care has to be taken not to burn the utensil, particularly since snow also acts as a blotter. This is the second reason why a few mouthfuls seem actually parching. The safest technique when you want to boil the kettle is to melt snow in small quantities until the bottom of the container is protected with several inches of water. You can then begin filling it with the greater quantities of snow usually necessary if anything like a capacity amount of liquid is desired.

These shortcomings are more than compensated for by the fact that snowfall makes water readily available throughout the woods, the mountains, the plains, and the desert it whitens. All one has to do is scoop up clean handfuls

Water from the wilderness lakes of the northern United States and Canada is usually pure, unless there are many camps on the shores or along the courses running into the lakes.

while walking along. The body requires a great deal more water in cold weather than most of us would ordinarily expect, for the kidneys then have to take over much of the process of elimination otherwise accomplished by the perspiration glands.

How to Simplify Dishwashing

Washing dishes is not really much of a chore if you have some system about it and if you always clean up immediately after a meal. With your cook kit, you'll find it helpful to include such items as a bar of laundry soap, two small tough dishcloths, a little dish mop, and scouring pads that combine steel wool with soap. While you are eating, have your largest kettle over the fire heating dishwater.

At the jump-off place, buy a cheap tin dishpan if you've the room and ditch it when the trip is over. This will not take up much space if you select a model into which other items in your outfit will nest.

If you prefer, however, you can take along a small canvas wash basin. Such a seven-ounce affair that one of us has carried for years is four inches high and twelve inches in diameter. It squashes down flat to pack. You can even get by with a square of plastic, digging a hole every time you want to use it, and pressing the plastic within to serve as the wash pan. If you're short on receptacles, fill this with water while the meal is cooking, drop in a few pebbles for insulators, and using a bent green stick as tongs, set in several large clean stones from the fire to heat the water. The tin basin, however, is handier than either of these.

Every fellow, as he finishes his meal, scrapes his plate into the fire. When you are through with the frypans, fill them with water and put on the fire to boil. Do the same with any kettle containing the sticky residue of mush.

Down at the creek or lake shore, you will find clusters of grass growing, with mud or sand adhering to the roots. Pull up a clump and use it to scour the outside of pots and also both the interior and exterior of the frypans before you wash them. Pans in which cereals like rolled oats have been cooked are particularly bothersome. If you will put a little square of butter or margarine in the water when you are preparing the cereal, it will make the pot ten times easier to clean.

If you have a pet aluminum pot, whose exterior you want to keep bright, coat the outside with a thick film of soap before you place it on the fire. All trace of black will then quickly wash off clean as a whistle. Eventually, most kettles get thoroughly darkened with soot on the outside, which sticks most tenaciously and which can scarcely be removed by anything short of steel wool. But this soot does no harm whatever and even makes food in such a kettle cook faster. If you scour the kettle with sand or muddy grass as sug-

Clean snow is a safe—and plentiful—thirst-quencher.

Washing up is an easy chore if you get at it right away.

gested, very little of the soot will rub off on other things when you pack. It is customary to have a canvas bag in which to stow the nest of kettles. This helps to keep them from blackening other articles in the outfit.

It has been the experience of a great many of the old sourdoughs in Alaska and the Northwest that when a utensil used for cooking meat is washed with soap, they get bad digestive disturbances akin to poisoning, and that indigestion ceases when such washing is stopped. One way to clean a steel frypan is to heat it very hot, then quickly plunge it into cold water. If this does not remove all the dirt, then scrub with sand and rinse in clear boiling water. Another way of loosening grease is to fill the pan with water into which some wood ashes have been dropped, and allow the whole thing to come to a boil beside the blaze.

Index

Boldface numbers refer to illustrations

A

B

C